Chica Lit

Latino and Latin American Profiles
Frederick Luis Aldama, Editor

Chica Lit

Popular Latina Fiction and Americanization in the
Twenty-First Century

Tace Hedrick

University of Pittsburgh Press

Published by the University of Pittsburgh Press, Pittsburgh, Pa., 15260
Copyright © 2015, University of Pittsburgh Press
All rights reserved
Manufactured in the United States of America
Printed on acid-free paper
10 9 8 7 6 5 4 3 2 1

ISBN 10: 0-8229-6365-5
ISBN 13: 978-0-8229-6365-3

Cataloging-in-Publication data is on file with the Library of Congress.

I dedicate this book to the memory of my parents, Bill and Lisa Hedrick, and to Bernardo Cárdenas, who has provided me with life and love.

Contents

Acknowledgments

This book would not exist if it were not for Frederick Aldama, and his kindness and cheer saw it to the finish line. I must also thank Iñyaki Rodeño, Suzanne Bost, and Frances Aparicio for giving me the opportunities to publish my initial work on chica lit. Pamela Gilbert and Kenneth Kidd gave me unwavering support on this project. Efraín Barradas unquestioningly had my back; Brigitte Aaron-Weltman and I shared many cups of tea over discussions of our work. My graduate students at the University of Florida, especially Gabriel Mayora, shared ideas and offered firm encouragement, as well as patience, while I finished writing. Judy Page, the director of Women's Studies at the University of Florida, gave me the administrative time off I needed to write. Arlene Dávila's work and her personal encouragement spurred me on. There are many others who assisted me in this work, too numerous to mention. Although their names are not here, I thank them also.

Preface

What's a Girl to Do When . . . ?

"The publishing industry expected us to be writing tales of oppression and exile and misery and all this sort of stuff they were
used to, and instead we were writing legitimately what our lives are
like," says Alisa Valdes-Rodriguez, the Albuquerque, N.M., author
who launched the chica-lit revolution three years ago with "The
Dirty Girls Social Club."

"I'm an Ivy League graduate, middle-class person who just lives
a regular American life—you know, born and raised here, don't
speak all that much Spanish—and there are lots and lots of people
like me."

—Kerry Lengel, "Hot Chica Lit Takes a Sassy
Style to Look at Latina Life"

At the beginning of Argentinian American Lara Rios's 2006 chica
lit fiction *Becoming Latina in Ten Easy Steps*, we learn that the Mexican American protagonist Marcela Alvarez (twenty-seven years old,
a successful movie animator) has never felt, as she puts it, "Latina"
enough for her family. (Confusingly, the book switches between
calling her "Latina," "Mexican," and "Mexican-American.") As she
woefully notes, "I've never been to Mexico, yet I feel disloyal when
I feel nothing at the sight of a waving Mexican flag. . . . My family
makes me crazy" (3). To make matters worse, in the next few pages,
we learn along with Marcela that she is not the biological daughter of
her Mexican father. Instead, she is the product of an affair between
an unknown white man and her Mexican American mother.[1] She decides that her newly discovered "white blood" is at fault for her not
being Latina enough, and constructs a list of ten things she must do to
remedy the problem, among them learning Spanish, learning how to
cook Mexican food, and most importantly finding a suitable Mexican
American boyfriend. Indeed, what's a girl to do when she's faced with
such a dilemma?

Yet at the crux of this narrative is actually another, more central question: How can Marcela stay American—that is, materially successful and culturally assimilated into the middle-class mainstream—and "become Latina" at the same time? Despite the title, *Becoming Latina* is structured to assure you, gentle reader, that giving up American values—having access to material wealth, being well educated, and obtaining the proper romantic relationship—will never be at issue.[2] In reality, Marcela and the reader must both learn, through Marcela's negative experiences as well as her positive ones, how she can properly Americanize her Mexican American heritage. In this sense, chica lit fiction like *Becoming Latina* can be read as examples of a long tradition of women's popular advice and behavior manuals. Alongside teaching the reader proper values and behavior as an American, however, chica lit must go further in that it teaches how ideas about what it means to be Mexican, for example, can be fashioned into a consumable source from which the initially confused chica will be able to accomplish both her romantic as well as professional goals. For instance, after several sexual (mis)adventures—at least one with a deeply unsuitable *vato loco* gangbanger—Marcela finds the successful, non–Spanish speaking Mexican American man of her dreams ("George, from accounting. . . . he dresses neat"). At the same time, she participates in the thoroughly American process of ethnic uplift by mentoring a feisty Mexican American barrio girl named Lupe Perez, and discovers her "roots" by learning to cook Mexican food with a private chef and embarking on a project at work to make an animated movie, called *Aztec Kings*, about Hernán Cortés's conquest of the Aztecs.

Fiction like *Becoming Latina*, written by US-born Latina and Mexican American authors and featuring young, upwardly mobile Latina protagonists, are part of a subgenre known as "chica lit." Chica lit is, as we will see, something of a niche market of chick lit, and itself connected by deep generic roots to the romance novel. These novels are, like the genre of chick lit to which they are related, most often peopled by young women who are (or, by the end of the book, will be) successful, educated professionals or businesswomen, with access to material wealth as well as totally cool wardrobes. Although some are successful at the beginning of the narrative, some chica lit heroines must go through trials and tribulations to attain their professions or businesses; all of them must go through some trouble in order to gain the right—at least for the moment—man. As far as this goes, think a Latina combination of *Bridget Jones's Diary* and *Sex and the City.*

Yet chica lit is chick lit with a complex and contradictory difference. Marcela's dilemma—how to mediate between her Americanness and her Mexican American heritage—is, unlike unmarked chick lit, which generally features young white women and assumes a white audience, a central aspect, indeed a requirement, for chica lit. Here, characters are constantly faced not only with a gendered but also with an often racialized ethnic crisis, posed as a dilemma of identity, which must, for the narrative to succeed on its many levels, ultimately be resolvable through the attainment of both romantic and professional success. The contradictions inherent in this presumed dilemma, however, are many, and begin to appear especially when the formula-driven narrative of chica lit cannot contain and most often cannot clearly define what exactly it means to become Latina within the boundaries of what it means to be "American." Yet it is also here where, as a feminist Latina/o studies scholar interested in contemporary representations of women in popular culture and popular genre fiction, I locate the study of chica lit within Latina/o studies more generally.

I first encountered chica lit in revising a 2010 course devoted to reading contemporary US Latina/Chicano literature. In particular, my eye was caught by Marta Acosta's *Happy Hour at Casa Dracula* (2008)—a madcap, clever paranormal romance with a Mexican American heroine—because I had recently taught a course in women's popular genre fiction and had included Stephenie Meyer's *Twilight* (2005). As I investigated further, I found that Acosta's book belonged to the category of chica lit. Reading some of the other titles—particularly Alisa Valdes-Rodriguez's *Dirty Girls Social Club* (published in 2003, the first of the chica lit fiction)—I decided that although these were not "good literature" in the academic sense, the fact of their popularity meant that they were important to the ways Latinos/Chicanas were represented, and represented themselves, in mass culture.

That I taught *Happy Hour* and *Dirty Girls* alongside other contemporary and well-received United States Latina/o novels, like Afro-Dominican-American writer Junot Díaz's *The Brief Wondrous Life of Oscar Wao* and *Days of Awe* by queer Cuban American author Achy

Obejas, may raise eyebrows among Latino studies scholars. Most work in this field, including mine, tends to emphasize resistance to the struggles, poverty, and inequalities that the majority of Latinos and Chicanas still face. Why, then, teach fiction that is clearly oriented toward a relatively small group of middle-class Latinas/os, who advocate the assimilation of Latinas and Chicanas into the gendered and racialized ideals of a neoliberal Americanization, and that seems to advocate, ultimately, the erasure of most subversive critical differences? At first, as I noted above, I simply wanted to investigate along with my students representations of Latina lives within the heavily mediated consumer culture where, in late modernity, we all make our home. Quickly I found that performing close readings of fiction such as this necessitated the critical eye of feminist and Latina studies in order to tease out the sometimes contradictory ideological positions in which these chicas found themselves. In addition, I began to understand that, just as with heavily mediated and consumer-oriented chick lit, or paranormal romance such as *Twilight*, I needed to use a methodology that would help my students and me to understand the various ideological shaping forces involved in the production of chica lit as a commodified product. Unlike *Twilight*, however, which allies itself to the love of whiteness and wealth via the narrative foil of poor Native American bodies, we also needed to understand the *function* of chica lit in a US cultural imaginary, itself invested in contradictory ideas about the race, ethnicity, and access to resources of Latinos and Chicanas. Thinking about chica lit's task in the production of vexed but important representations by and of Latinas and Chicanos allows us to understand also how they fit into these presumably breezy, light "beach reads."

These readings will help scholars as well as students and readers at large to situate the easily consumed nature and often conservative politics of chica lit within a more complex landscape of literary and cultural imaginings about, and self-representations of, Latinas/Chicanos. As part of the negotiations involved when marginalized peoples must constantly rethink and reimagine what it means to be able to lead a "regular American life," the study of chica lit adds another dimension to the broad range of Latina/o studies.

Chica Lit

Introduction

A Regular American Life

> Within current debates about race and difference, mass culture is
> the contemporary location that both publicly declares and perpet-
> uates the idea that there is pleasure to be found in the acknowl-
> edgement and enjoyment of racial difference. . . . Within commod-
> ity culture, ethnicity becomes spice, seasoning that can liven up
> the dull dish that is mainstream white culture.
> —BELL HOOKS, "EATING THE OTHER: DESIRE AND RESISTANCE"

This book is an examination of a niche market in contemporary US
women's popular fiction called "chica lit." It is a growing niche—since
the publication of *Dirty Girls*, publisher's imprints such as St. Martin's
Griffin, HarperCollins's series Avon Trade, Penguin's Berkley Books,
Grand Central Station, and others have put out an increasing number of chica lit fictions. As writing about Latina characters by Latina
authors, it would seem that chica lit should be included within the
parameters of US Latina/o literature. However, chica lit deliberately
follows a good many of the "beach read" conventions of the hugely
successful, commercially oriented chick lit and romance publishing
markets. Because of this, chica lit's representations of mostly middle-
class Latina characters, in mass-market form, guarantees that these
novels' overt class strivings and conservative ideological underpin-
nings are quite different even from many popular Latina/o writers
who now publish in large mainstream presses, such as Junot Díaz,
Sandra Cisneros, or Cristina García. Indeed, as Catherine Ramírez

1

asserts, chica lit, "like so many other narratives in and about the United States, fuse[s] wealth and Americanization" (24). As with the academic study of popular and mass-market women's writing, which has had to defend itself from charges that its object of study is too consumer-oriented and not "literary," the relatively small number of Latina/o studies analyses of chica lit demonstrates that its commercialism and seemingly "lite" content elicit much the same academic reaction in Latina/o studies. At the same time, prominent Latina/o studies scholars across disciplines, such as literary scholar Elena Sáez and anthropologist Arlene Dávila, have shown the ways that commodified representations of a gendered and raced *latinidad* constitute an integral share of what it means to "be Latina/o" in the US social imaginary; chica lit belongs in this signifying space. I place chica lit at the intersection of genre constraints, the marketing of ethnicity at the neoliberal turn of the century, the mainstreaming of Latina/o difference into what Erin Hurt calls a "common American sameness," and the concomitant demonization of Latino poverty (134).[1]

Changes in US demographics in the last twenty years, particularly for US Latinos/as and Mexican Americans, have pushed the marketing strategies of mainstream popular women's genre publishing to open up a small but important new arena of Latina/o writing. Chica lit might not exist, in fact, without the so-called "Latino explosion" of the mid to late 1990s and beyond, when census figures and marketing demographics were touted as evidence that Latinos had arrived on the (commercial) scene, giving rise to the aggressive marketing of "Latino" products, music, food, and dance. The hype was media-driven, and tended to privilege East Coast Latinos/as whose original national cultures derived more from the Hispanophone Caribbean than from Mexico or Central and South America. Speaking of the apex of this period, Agustín Gurza notes,

> It began with Puerto Rican heartthrob Ricky Martin smiling and shimmying his way to the top of the pop charts with the sinuous "Livin' la Vida Loca," a sensual smash hit that came to symbolize the frenzied cultural breakthrough of a long-marginalized minority. . . . But Ricky wasn't alone that year. There were J. Lo and Marc Anthony, two native Nuyoricans from Latino barrios. There was Miami's Enrique Iglesias, privileged son of the suave Spanish pop

star. There was Carlos Santana and then Christina Aguilera. And in the wings, studying her English, was Shakira, the Lebanese Colombian who would soon seduce the world with her belly dance and her charming accent. Never before had so many Latinos spent so much time at the top of the pop charts in a single year. (Gurza)

In this 2004 essay Gurza takes a look back and opines that the Latino explosion disappeared like a flash in the pan. However, the attention paid by marketers and demographers to the growing Latino presence in the United States has in fact continued, though possibly not at such a fever pitch. Yet as Gurza argues, the homogenized "Latinization" of an extremely varied US Latino ethnicity—often imagined in the United States as a singular entity—guarantees that Latina products such as chica lit are dependent on a homogenized set of marketing assumptions about "Latino culture." Although these assumptions are presented as marketing verities, they tend to reflect social imaginaries about what it means to be Latina/o.[2] Interestingly, it can be argued that the space for the beginnings of "ethnic" chick lit began to be carved out first by Terry McMillan's third and extremely successful novel *Waiting to Exhale*, published in 1992. This novel served as something of a precursor to white, chick lit "girlfriend" narratives such as Candace Bushnell's *New York Observer* column and subsequent novel, television series, and two movies. But *Waiting to Exhale* not only introduced the question of race into the romance/financial success formula, it paved the way for publishers to be on the lookout for other ethnic book markets and authors. Publishers such as St. Martin's Press and Penguin Books were poised to leap upon the first inkling that such a book was in the works—as became the case with Valdes's *Dirty Girls*. These publishers had been primed by the widespread agreement, itself fueled by marketers' and media's reading of the 1990 and 2000 censuses, that these two decades would be the time of the "Latino explosion" when "Hispanics" would become the next great market in the United States.

At the time of this writing, chica lit is still very young; its beginning can be dated to the publication in 2003 of Alisa Valdes-Rodriguez's book *The Dirty Girls Social Club*, often hailed, in fact, in the publishing industry as the "Latina" *Waiting to Exhale*. This niche category of women's fiction,[3] whose closest cousins are white and African American chick lit and contemporary romance fiction, consists of books written by self-proclaimed assimilated US Latina and Mexican American authors, featuring young, twenty to thirty-year-old, upwardly mobile or already middle-class Latina or Mexican American strivers and arrivers. Popular media coined the term "chica lit," although the publishing industry itself does not label such fiction this way; on publishing websites one can usually find chica lit listed under a general fiction heading, or sometimes, more rarely, in Latina romance. In fact, somewhere on the back cover, most publishers simply list their chica lit books as "fiction."[4] Yet the name has stayed, and the ability of readers, interviewers, and reviewers to identify which books are chica lit is usually unchallenged, although scholars and reviewers will occasionally use the phrase "Latina chick lit." Indeed, as close relation to romance fiction and chick lit, chica lit also has strong historical, publishing, and genre connections to other popular women's writing, including coming-of-age, paranormal romance, and "career girl" fiction.

I began this introduction with a description of chica lit as it appears in the marketplace precisely because it is a mass-marketed, generic product (in the sense of belonging to one or more genres). Every scholar of chica lit has taken note of this fact to one extent or another, mostly in essays devoted to the work of Alisa Valdes. As Erin Hurt has noted of *Dirty Girls*, "This novel marks a turning point for Latina/o literature and criticism by raising questions about what Latina identity is and how we conceptualize it. *The Dirty Girls Social Club* ultimately upsets the traditional critical paradigm of reading Latina literary works in terms of their oppositional consciousness and asks how genre and the marketplace can shape a text's cultural work" (134). I take Hurt's suggestion that chica lit must be examined in terms of the requirements and exigencies of publishing and marketing popular women's fiction together with the often knotty problem of how to safely represent, within the confines of mass marketing, a Latina ethnicity among the minefields of contradictory discourses about Latinos, immigration, and "Americanness." Here, chica lit functions as a form of advice or behavior manual for the cultural Americanization of young Latinas, both strivers and arrivers. As an overarching approach, I place the production of chica lit, and the ways it markets a Latina middle-class subjectivity, within late twentieth- and early twenty-first-century socioeconomic changes in the United States. As we will see, many Latina/Chicano critics of the US commodification of ethnicity define such changes under the rubric of neoliberalism.

NEOLIBERALISM AND NARRATIVE

Scholars of cultural studies, literary studies, and anthropology such as Arlene Dávila, Frances Negrón-Muntaner, Elena Sáez-Machado, and Kristy Ulibarri assert that alterations in the social representation of, and by, Latinos have come about as a result of shifts in social and cultural outlooks that have accompanied the adoption of economic neoliberalism, beginning in the latter part of the 1970s. Ulibarri's examination of neoliberalism in the shaping of Latina/Chicano literature from the 1970s forward argues that the popular notion of neoliberalism as a "new" socioeconomic order is something of a misnomer, since its elements do not constitute an entirely new socioeconomic vision. Neoliberalism's antecedents come both from a nineteenth-century classical liberalism that advocated less government in the economy and from a reaction to Keynesian "embedded liberalism" where the state "is given free rein within the market" (152). Such an outlook, as she notes, responds to its antecedents in privileging privatization and in its emphasis on a combination of individualized effort and self-correcting markets, rather than an acknowledgment of the structural aspects of socioeconomic barriers (153). Rather, neoliberalism is "a transformation (both ideologically and pragmatically) of the relationship between social relations and market objectives," ones that favor state deregulation as a way toward "developing more proficient (and less bureaucratic) government" (152). Arguments about the ways a neoliberal outlook frames contemporary discourses about the class, cultural, and citizenship status of Latinos centers on the (seemingly) unintended consequences of what came to be called the "Washington consensus." Although this so-called consensus was initially laid out in relationship to the debt crisis in Latin America in the 1980s, the neoliberal policies set out have slowly but surely been espoused as economic verities north of the border, with the result that many neoliberal policies have been put into practice not just in Latin America but also in the United States itself. Most importantly, these have included, over the long run, a fundamental shift in the United States not just in governmental policies but in popular attitudes toward and representations of wealth and its accumulation, as well as the place of the (publishing) market in the social lives and imaginaries of consumers.[5] In this sense, as Ulibarri puts it, "Latino/a literature . . . is both contestatory and in contestation, where it resists the appropriations and homogeneity of the market but finds itself fulfilling the market's desires for difference and niches." Using a selection of post-1970s Latina/o literature as examples, she shows how this writing "represents and emblematizes Latinos/as in this socioeconomic climate" (155).

As part of her argument, Ulibarri cites sociocultural anthropologist Aiwha Ong's work on the place of neoliberal practices in social life. Neoliberalist views, according to Ong, recast "politics as mainly a problematizing activity, one that shifts the focus away from social conflicts and toward the management of social life" (204–5). In this sense, Ulibarri maintains, "neoliberalism [is] the major framework in which social relations are shaped" (154). Such shaping has moved government policies aimed at redressing social problems away from Lyndon Johnson's "War on Poverty" in the 1960s and '70s, and toward, by the end of the 1980s, a view that poverty in particular is, if not remedied by market forces, then inevitable. Thus, some of the same policies of neoliberalism as had been forcibly reshaping Latin American economies during their debt crises—codified in what is loosely known as the "Washington consensus"—have been adapted through the turn of the century in socioeconomic practices in the United States.[6] Particularly important for my argument here, these scholars and others have discussed the role of poverty in neoliberal viewpoints. Arlene Dávila, for example, has documented how this framework has resulted in what she calls the "fall from grace" of poverty as a policy issue, and the rise of a policy and media emphasis on Latino upward mobility and celebratory representations of a Latino middle class (33–34).

In her *Latino Spin: Public Image and the Whitewashing of Race* (2008), Dávila pays close attention to a relatively new vision of middle-class Latinos as possessing American cultural citizenship. This discourse has at least in part been produced and reproduced by marketing interests, anxious to respond to the "growing xenophobia that envelops discussion of Latino immigrants which, extending to all Latinos, demands their continued sanitation through positive commercial images" (73). In unraveling some of the complications and paradoxes that make up US representations of Latino/a class status, she notes that two authors of the 1980s and '90s in particular stimulated discussion about the image of Latinos as a monolithic "imagined working-class community" (31). These were Richard Rodriguez, whose *Hunger of Memory* came out in 1982, and Linda Chávez, with her *Out of the Barrio: Toward a New Politics of Hispanic Assimilation* of 1991. As Dávila points out, "Both espoused the view that empowerment can only come through assimilation, and both censure Latinos' culture and the Spanish language as culprits for their ghettoization" (32). Although immediately controversial, such writers opened "discussion on the Latino middle class throughout the 1990s," when it began to be the case that the very middle-class status of most "Latino researchers, journalists, and other Latinologists speaking for or on behalf of Latinos" produced a revisionary narrative of the middle-class Latino.

Finally, she notes, the marketing industry, picking up on such narratives, "has been a leading force in projecting Latinos' buying power and their middle-class status" (26), and points to the ways corporate interests have begun either commissioning or using academic and think-tank research on middle-class Latinos. These efforts are not completely without precedence, but what is new about them in the twenty-first century is the "growing importance of the corporate sector. . . . [and] the larger political and economic context favoring emphasis on upwardly mobile constituencies, at the cost of the working poor" (28). The over-celebratory nature of public and mass media discussions of the "rise" of a Latino middle class functions to put under erasure the fact that, as a group, Latinos "are still overwhelmingly working- and lower-middle class, [and] that [Latino/a] poor almost tripled during the same time there was a growth in the Latino middle class" (29). Such chica lit celebrations of Latina/o success, and their concomitant demonization of Latino poverty, are central to what Dávila has identified as a middle-class Latino "corrective" to the idea of Latinos/as as "monolithically working-class," an image "in which [Latino middle-class researchers] simply do not recognize themselves, and that many blame for their subordination" (*Latino Spin* 32). Such a corrective impulse, as I will argue, forms a central aspect of the motivations toward the didacticism of chica lit itself.

The marketing orientation and narrative content of chica lit, focusing on well-educated and upwardly mobile Latina characters, indicates that the ideal chica lit audience that publishers and authors imagine is also, or at least aspires to be, middle-class. Given chica lit's strong emphasis on material success and cultural Americaniza- tion, the ideal audience would also seem to consist of young US-born Latinas who are negatively invested in what they view as out-of-date, clichéd, or stereotyped notions of "authentic" and therefore resistant, or cultural nationalist, ethnicity. As Ellen McCracken suggests, au- thors like Valdes "want to have it both ways—she both plays on stereo- types of Latina/o ethnicity and debunks them. . . . [her] chatty, col- loquial language—designed to make readers feel part of a group of friends—takes a distance . . . from stereotypes of Latinas, precisely as it invokes these motifs to flavor the novel" ("From Chapbooks to Chica Lit" 17-18). Chica lit novels, then, balance awkwardly between rejecting racialized and classed stereotypes at the same time that such images help to do the difficult textual work of inserting, by way of foregrounding and contrast, their heroines' American values and (eventual) access to middle-class capital into genre elements that, un- less otherwise marked, assume whiteness.

CONVENTIONS AND GENRES

Chica lit expresses contemporary US fears and desires about the lives of Latinas through genre conventions, or elements, which are inex- tricably linked by now with mass-market production. These conven- tions—forming narrative patterns found in genre fiction ranging from contemporary romance to chick lit—are the parts of the textual ma- chine from which the story must be built. Such constraints derive first from chica lit's relationship with the plot conventions, or formulae, of other popular women's genres, which include, in particular, close ties to the romance novel as well as to its more recent sister genre, chick lit. As Dirk de Geest and An Goris note of the language used in romance writers' handbooks, "Whereas traditional constraints are mainly in- tended to function as creative stimuli, the constraints pertaining to popular literature always (implicitly or explicitly) operate under the understanding that publication and commercial success are (part of) their ultimate goal. As a result, the economic, commercial, and insti- tutional frameworks surrounding popular genres such as the romance novel constantly influence the formulation of their norms, despite the fact that the illusion of writing as a free and autonomous creative activity is maintained throughout the handbooks" (82). The second set of limitations, linked equally to popular genre production as to mass-market requirements, is the ambiguous and ambivalent nature of the term "Latina." The genre-specific aspects of the books themselves, and the efforts of publishers' marketing strategies, work to pare down received ideas about the "Latina" to a binary of stereotype or success. Yet the enormous complexities of Latino/Chicana lives and experiences in the United States, coupled with often paradoxical popular assumptions about Latinos and Chicanas, consistently undermine the very need, on the part of publishing houses, to pin down the proper marketing niche in which to place chica lit. In this sense, the apparently excessive nature of Latina/o subjectivity seems to escape chica lit's genre and publishing constraints.

Thus, these novels pose an often vexed central question of how exactly their characters fit what might be considered "ethnic" qualities into a successful performance of a certain classed and gendered Americanness.[7] Such contradictions must be contained, and chica lit works to accomplish this in part by employing the convention of the dilemma and its resolution. That is, questions of race, poverty, and sexism are first shaped as private conflicts or dilemmas for the chica heroine, but depend on the notion that such conflicts are always ultimately resolvable. This generic structure is, of course, necessary in order to push the narrative over its potentially awkward humps and onward to its satisfactory resolution.

Thus, chica lit needs (happy) resolutions, not just to its characters' plot-driven dilemmas, but to deal with the inevitable contradictions produced by fitting Latinas, in all their racial, cultural, and class differences and representations, into conventions originally developed mostly around the representations of white, middle-class women. Part and parcel of the convention of the resolvable conflict has to do with the apparent transparency of the writing—the didactic mode being so familiar to women as to seem like a natural means of communication—and the apparent "relatability" of its situations and characters to the reader. As Janice Radway notes of the romance readers with whom she worked, "Even though the Smithton women know the stories are improbable, they also assume that the world that serves as the backdrop for those stories is exactly congruent with their own" (109).

Through the chica lit plot, not merely fantastic but actual (if often improbable) possibilities adorn the relatability and congruency of the characters and situations to the reader's own life and world.

Like romance and chick lit novels, chica lit characters and their backgrounds often involve many references to the real world of young women's personal experiences with men, money, body image, and careers. The world of chica lit is also made to seem congruent with that of its readers via fixtures of real life, crowding the fictional scene with instantly recognizable references to real-world brands, corporate structures, and uses of technology such as blogs, e-mail, and Facebook. These stories' endings, as fantastic as they often are, must nevertheless offer some points of congruence with the woman reader's own world so that their promise is always possible and characters relatable, no matter how unlikely. For example, as we will see in further detail, Marta Acosta's third novel in her *Casa Dracula* quartet strategizes her Mexican American character Milagro's too-ethnic taste within the boundaries of media marketing that shapes the real (corporate) world of bridal and wedding preparations. The "reality factor" in this case is itself made up of appeals to a fantasy world created and sustained by reality television, print, and online media. Such a backdrop is especially easy for Acosta to use, since so many products aimed at women—from movies to magazines to television—present these very same "dreams" and fantasies as attainable realities (my own dirty little viewing secret, TLC's *Say Yes to the Dress*, has been seductive for me in just this fashion). Thus, the Latina reader can relate to the Latina character placed in such familiar situations, surroundings, and desires: "That *could* be me," no matter how unlikely.

Thus, at the same time that these narrative conclusions often dissolve into impossible fantasies of romance and success, chica lit—like romance and chick lit—must by its very nature also present situations and characters that seem "true to life" for its readers. Actual dilemmas of structural racism, sexism, and socioeconomic class position may be raised for the sake of relatability, but also must be presented as private and individual, overcome by the character's own spunky nature and the lessons she has learned in her journey toward romance and material well-being. In this sense, both the pleasure and the ease of reading chica lit, and its packaging as a throwaway "beach read" mean, if the testimony of my own students is anything to go on, that the didactic and prescriptive functions of romance, chick lit, and chica lit will for the most part go unnoticed, though they are not inactive.[8]

ADVICE AND AMERICANIZATION

The publishing and genre requirements within which chica lit is written and marketed demand a particular analytical framework that takes into account chica lit's place in the US history of popular, mass-market women's writing. Just as importantly, as I noted in my preface, any analysis of chica lit must attend to its central concern: how to "do" a recognizable ethnicity while clearly embodying the cultural requirements for being "American" in the early twenty-first century. In other words, this reading must also parse out chica lit's contributions to often contradictory representations and beliefs about the presumed Americanness of the Latina/o subject. In this sense, chica lit attempts to lay out, in narrative form, prescriptions for attaining an American cultural citizenship for upwardly mobile Latinas, one that gestures toward a kind of "value-added" model of legal citizenship.[9] Cultural citizenship assumes that legal citizenship is not enough to make one appear to be, or even to feel, fully part of the nation; as Renato Rosaldo explains, the cultural aspect of citizenship uses "cultural expression to claim public rights and recognition" (35), especially when such recognition and its attendant rights are in question. In this sense, my earlier assertion (see preface) of Marcela's Americanization is only seemingly at odds with the book's title, *Becoming Latina*. At the end of this narrative, Marcela is clearly and finally delineated as "American": legally a US citizen, of course, and patriotic, yes. But she has also figured out how to craft a "Mexican" heritage into material, romantic, and even social success. She does so by working on her own animated movie about Cortéz, marrying a middle-class Mexican American, George (not Jorge), who works in accounting, and engaging in the "uplift" of a barrio Mexican American, Lupe Perez, who will in Lara Rios's next book go to college and write a thesis called "Being Americana." Interestingly, the most obvious solution—that Marcela could actually go to Mexico and explore her "heritage" there—seemingly constitutes a danger in chica lit generally, not merely to the Americanization of these young women but to their becoming Latina in a correct manner. In only two of the twelve books I examine here will the idea to visit a Latin American or Caribbean country of origin even occur to any of the characters. For the chica heroine to become, and remain, culturally American, these narratives must take place *within the boundaries* of the United States. Yet if, as happens occasionally, the chica heroine is located, for whatever amount of time, into the greater Hispanophone Americas, she must then be relocated quickly back to the States and the journey constituted as a necessary step on the path to the happy ending.

These books' insistence on cultural enfranchisement as an American exceeds the fact that their characters are legally American by birth; in other words, there is something about the Latina or Mexican American subject that continues to be seen as "foreign," that is, not American. This was already evident in Americanization discourses of the 1920s, directed especially at women who were already Mexican Americans, particularly in border states such as California and Texas. As George Sánchez has shown, women were the target of these campaigns, and when older Mexican immigrant women "proved difficult to Americanize, these programs focused their efforts on the adolescent American-born Chicana" (Sánchez 476). Sánchez begins, indeed, by quoting an Americanization teacher of Mexican and second-generation Mexican American women, who wrote in 1923 that "the Americanization of the women is as important a part as that of the men. They are harder to reach but more easily educated. . . . The children of these foreigners are the advantages to America, not the naturalized foreigners. These are never 100% Americans, but the second generation may be. 'Go after the women' and you may save the second generation for America" (476). Both its "corrective" impulses against "stereotypes" of Latino poverty and un-American activities, and chica lit's connection to other prescriptive and didactic genres such as chick lit and romance novels, illuminate these novels as behavior manuals, teaching and informing their readers proper American values. Just as Americanization campaigns needed instruction or advice manuals to "go after the women," chica lit does the same. As Caroline Smith shows, chick lit in general—and here I include chica lit—is engaged with what she calls the "consumer culture medium" of advice for women, referring outside their own pages to real or thinly disguised magazines, columns, television shows, and romantic comedies aimed at women. As she notes, "these mediums heavily influence the protagonists . . . dictating to them expected feminine ideals and behaviors that they should attempt to achieve" (5). References to real-life women's advice media—such as *Dirty Girls*'s Rebecca's ownership of the women's magazine *Ella*, an allusion to the magazine *Latina*—chica lit itself acts as late modern women's advice literature. In this sense, chica lit presents solutions not merely to women's problems about friends, careers, and romance but also specifically to legally and generationally American, assimilated Latinas whose ethnicity nevertheless raises suspicions about their American identities. As we will see, chica lit's didactic undertones and class-oriented corrective narratives show its readers, through the trials and ultimate triumphs of chica characters carefully drawn so as to appear "relatable" to real-world lives, how to incorporate a largely imagined Latina or Mexican American cultural heritage into what Lara Rios calls "being Americana."

Chica lit thus functions as a teaching device about the proper use of ethnicity in middle-class women's lives, producing a normalized and, as far as possible, *unmarked* ethnic identity constructed by participation in both the presumably private world of romance and, importantly, the public world of business and careers. Chica lit advice on such matters, indeed, looks much like that which is packaged and merchandised, for example, in the pages of *Latina* magazine.[10] How chica lit presents its lessons on achieving the Americanness of a "regular" life, and what sorts of behaviors, knowledges, sacrifices and, of course, rewards this life entails for both chica lit authors and their characters, are questions I address in this book.

Although we usually think of nineteenth-century romance, often addressed to its "dear reader," as the epitome of the authorial, didactic narrative, such "teacherly" modes are still, at the beginning of the twenty-first century in the United States, central to a vast array of products marketed both for and by women. Women might indeed be said to be habituated to the advice form, easily found as it is even in the checkout lane at the grocery, where the pages of women's magazines offer their readers a wealth of information—and advice on how to properly use such knowledge—on a seemingly infinite array of problems and pleasures. Women's popular novels, too, provide information and instruction. As Janice Radway writes in her now classic *Reading the Romance* (1984), "instruction is one of the principle functions books can perform for their readers" (109). Indeed, Radway found that her readers had "faith in the reliability of mimesis" to the extent that, as she put it, "the value of the romance novel is a function of the information it is thought to contain . . . this information [is] a highly valued commodity in the advanced industrial society of which [the readers] are a part" (107). Some of the best work on this subject comes from scholarship on the historical connections between women's advice manuals and women's writing.

The linked genres of domestic, romance, and chick lit have long provided their readers with a sentimental education in "received ideas," romantic notions, and lessons for behavior. It has also served, according to Nancy Armstrong, in the (re)production of nation and class, particularly in the shaping of the notion of "separate spheres." Throughout the Americas writers often employed the sentimental and/or domestic novel in imagining—and didactically shaping—an emerging national, racial, and gendered modernity. As Doris Sommer demonstrates so aptly in her now classic *Foundational Fictions*, the nineteenth- and early twentieth-century Latin American sentimental novel (written, interestingly, mostly by men) couched racial and sexual union as metaphors for the formation of the new Latin American nation. Both Latin American and British sentimental fiction were important to the shaping of the modern nation when questions of class and gender demanded the delineation of new class systems as well as, for women of means, the construction and maintenance of a "domestic sphere" shaped as separate from the "public sphere." As Armstrong argues, such "spheres" are born in the realm of ideological discourses as they are constructed as material realities: "modern institutional cultures depend upon the separation of 'the political' from 'the personal' and . . . they *produce* and maintain this separation on the basis of gender. . . . [E]ven as certain forms of cultural information were separated into these two opposing fields, *they were brought together* as an intricate set of pressures that operated on the subject's body and mind to induce self-regulation" ("Some Call it Fiction" 578, my emphasis). The ways these presumably separate "spheres" have been constructed as such in the twenty-first century United States are to some extent quite different from the earlier fiction both Sommer and Armstrong discuss. Nevertheless, with its simultaneous emphasis on the public nature of a woman's individual style and her professional attainments, coupled with the idea that young women must once again be taught how to create the domestic nature of home and romance, chica lit also brings two seemingly "opposing fields" together. This process itself, narrativized, functions as a teacherly guide for the proper knowledge, methods, and behaviors in fully becoming Americanized.

Popular press reviews have praised chica lit like *Dirty Girls Social* Club for its apparently non-didactic tone, an observation that only makes sense if we understand two things. First, ethnic fiction is assumed to be both didactic and, usually, a "downer" in its representations of poor, working-class, and oppressed Latino and Chicana characters. Second, chica lit's opposite tactic of marketing itself as mere entertainment, and representing its characters as being "normal" in their problems and desires, reframes readers' expectations that its ethnic focus will be preachy, hectoring, or depressing. Yet a close look reveals those recurring elements of chica lit that are clearly meant to be informative: for example, Valdes's characters, such as Lauren, repeat the refrain "Did you know that. . . . ?" followed by factoids about Latinos and Latin Americans. In addition, chica lit clearly demonstrates, by negative examples of the "culture of poverty" and invidious comparisons with "old school" Chicano nationalism, what *not* to do and how *not* to perform cultural Americanization. These didactic and advice-giving elements come by way of overtly didactic sentimental novels and their skeletal but still discernable outlines in romance and chick lit fictions, updated for the perceived needs of middle-class US Latinas at the turn of the century (Ramírez 26).[11] The adoption of the advice manual in the form of a didactic narrative has its own history; here, it serves two ends for chica lit. First, the ubiquitous nature even today of advice for women constitutes a familiar and, because familiar, comforting and even pleasurable framework of information and instruction. Secondly, the ways in which advice and teaching for women is delivered provides a framework for the desire to provide a "corrective" to those "stereotypical" beliefs about Latinos' and Mexican Americans' poverty, resistance to middle-class values, and lack of ambition. Indeed, Ramírez's essay on *Dirty Girls* gives evidence through her discussion of readers' online comments that readers of chica lit feel that they have been both educated and recognized. Non-Latina readers report learning what it's like to "be a Latina," while self-identified Latina readers have reported that chica lit is both mimetic and relatable, in that they "see themselves" in its pages (15–16).

The production of advice manuals for women in the first part of the 1800s was not centered only in the United States and Britain, but appeared wherever there were (usually privileged) women who could read, for example in Mexico.[12] Especially in the United States, however, these advice manuals bear a close relationship to popular women's novels, one that continues all the way through the twenty-first century, with changing emphases depending on audience and time period.[13] In her study of chick lit, Caroline Smith notes that references to both fictive and actual women's advice manuals published since the 1980s (such as *The Rules*) appear often within the pages of chick lit fictions. She goes on to extend her definition of what constitutes advice manuals to chick lit mentions of women's "lifestyle" and decorating magazines, catalogues such as those put out by Williams-Sonoma, Martha Stewart shows and magazines, and even references to romantic comedies (5). Chica lit, with its emphasis on the (re)creation of a properly modern American Latina, would seem to have few specifically "Latina advice manuals" to fall back on. Yet drives for the Americanization especially of Mexican girls and women in the first part of the twentieth century— particularly in the 1920s and '30s—did produce domestic advice manuals that were at the same time explicitly about helping them to adjust to becoming, and being, American.[14] As we have seen, women were early on considered the best bet for getting ethnic—particularly Mexican— families Americanized. With anxieties and debates over migration from south of the US borders reaching much the same key pitch as they did in the first part of the twentieth century, around the immigration of Northern and Eastern Europeans, normalizing and Americanizing efforts have appeared once again, this time in the work of Latina/o writers, editors, and magazines.

In this context, the prescriptive aspects of chica lit have their roots, so to speak, in such seemingly non–chica lit places as governmental policy papers that examine the relatively small number of Latinos who have achieved middle-class success. These studies, as Dávila has shown, have trickled down from their origins into marketing strategies and into media headlines as well as into representations of Latinas in the entertainment industry (*Latino Spin* 32). More importantly for chica lit readers, these descriptions, and their implicit prescriptive nature, for the attainment of such a life are laid out as well in the articles and advertisements of lifestyle-oriented print and online magazines, from

Guanabee.com and UrbanLatino.com[15] to the much more serious fare in HispanicBusiness.com. The media conglomerate Batanga touts its website iMujer.com, for example, as the "premier lifestyle destination for Latinas looking to empower themselves with day-to-day solutions and information that allows them to be the woman they aspire to be" ("Hispanic Fact Pack"). Finally, the *Latina* print magazine, whose publishers also produce the middle-class African American magazine *Essence*, has been instrumental within the pages of chica lit—*Dirty Girls*'s New Mexican character Rebecca, for example, owns and publishes *Ella*, a thin disguise for *Latina*. Additionally, *Latina* itself has provided an important forum for chica lit, including sections from soon-to-be published books and interviews with authors. Like women's magazines, the informative aspects of the chica lit narrative can run the gamut of topics from bulimia, alcoholism, autism, rape, fashion, and style, to the dangers of men and poverty, to taste and class.

The didactic project of chica lit involves raising and then managing the anxieties of inhabiting a gendered, ethnic, and racialized identity, which is itself the focus of a vexed and often contradictory set of discourses of fear and desire in the United States. To this end, chica lit must work to shape, both through narrative and through genre formula, the social imaginary of a nonthreatening, middle-class "American Latina." Because chica lit itself participates in the same project of addressing—interpellating, in the French philosopher Louis Althusser's sense of calling forth—what Armstrong calls "bourgeois femininity," as she shows such middle-class femininity is "constructed through the domestic fictions that represent it as already in place" ("Some Call it Fiction" 579). Radway echoes this conclusion, noting that "the romance is not merely the analogical representation of a preexisting sensibility but a positive agent in its creation and perpetuation" (149–51). In much the same way, chica lit assures its readers through the very representation of such a subject that such a properly modern and American chica already exists. Using formulaic strategies concerned with work and romance borrowed from other genres, chica lit also reassures its reader that she too can and will embody this ethnic, American, and properly feminine subjectivity, so infinitely to be desired.

Yet there are, of course, some fundamental differences between chica lit and earlier didactic novels for women. Like contemporary romance and chick lit, each chica lit fiction makes sure that there is no doubt in the main character's mind that she will be, even if it is in the unexpressed "future" of the novel, happily settled in a well-monetized heterosexual coupledom at the same time that she is convinced of her right to sexual and financial independence. These freedoms, installed through the efforts of Women's Liberation and feminist movements in general, have been recast at the turn of the century in popular media so as to be deeply anxiety provoking: how to be successfully single, professional, and "fun," while still remaining active in the marriage market. How to "have it all" as mother, wife, and professional. Even more problematic, especially for chica lit written after the Great Recession, how, as a Mexican American, Cuban American, or Puerto Rican chica, does one attain the high level of financial success these novels seem almost inevitably to require?

Popular women's writing in general, as we saw in Armstrong's work, "induces self-regulation." However, lessons in self-regulation are no good unless they reach their intended audience. Thus, chica lit's narrative strategies and formulae are intrinsically part of a (increasingly online and digital) publishing and entertainment "machine" that ensures the rapid production of easily consumable niche-market texts. The formulaic plot and narrative lines between novels like chica lit and other women's popular genres, produced in the marketplace of "fast fiction"—that is, fiction meant to be produced and consumed at a quick rate—have become increasingly blurred. The pace of production and, especially, consumption of women's fiction in particular has contributed to this blurring of genres. Presses that publish genre fiction have also worked on the venue side of publishing in creating new and ever more convenient means and locations for selling their books quickly and cheaply.[16] Now, in the second decade of the twenty-first century, the ease and most especially the privacy (for loving romance novels or their cousins, chick or chica lit fiction, can still be for women a matter of some shame) of purchasing books on e-publishing platforms has also opened up a world of fast accessibility.

Fast Fiction

Scholars of women's popular fiction in the United States have long argued both for the serious study of women's popular literature and for historicizing the financial success and influence women authors of popular genres have had.[17] Although Ellen McCracken argues that Latina literature in general "is now almost completely structured by the demands of consumerism" ("Postmodern Continuum" 166), genre fiction specifically written for women has been structured by such demands for more than a century. Thus, it is important to note the ways that women who write popular fiction understand their writing as a business: not merely writing on a schedule, but knowing one's audience, negotiating with those who have the means of book production, and the necessity of self-promotion. Some authors embrace this understanding, but others do not. In an e-mail interview, Marta Acosta reveals her displeasure with this commercial aspect: "I am not a businesswoman. I am a writer and I resent all the business required to survive as a writer."

If women's easy access to popular fiction has come to symbolize (a bit of) pleasure and, even more importantly, some leisure to its readers, the making of such fiction is not so leisurely. The successful sales of romances, chick lit, and chica lit all depend on fast writing, quick production, brand-name recognition, and a publishing industry that demands that its authors, for the most part, do their own publicity. The "fast fiction" of chica lit as well as chick lit, then, works best when it is tied, as Aldama has noted, to "the formulaic romance genre," where an author can quickly hang her narrative on the framework of the familiar, tried-and-true conventions of the genre (*Routledge Concise History* 129). The use of the conventions of romance and its many subgenres also provide chica lit authors with a ready-made audience eager to snap up new, "fresh" popular fiction, which nevertheless iterates long-familiar lessons and pleasures.

Deliberately unlike Latina/Chicano writing canonized within academic Latina/o Studies, which often envisions a resistant ethnic and raced subjectivity, chica lit then, belongs squarely—even if, in some ways, uncomfortably—as a commodified artifact in an increasingly fast-paced publishing world, despite (or perhaps because) of its emphasis simultaneously on feminine sameness and ethnic difference. As McCracken maintains, the commodification and even canonization of specific Latina authors has been "framed, preceded by, and already shaped to a certain degree by the dominant discursive optic of multiculturalism" at work in a predominantly neoliberal US socioeconomic moment (*New Latina Narrative* 6). Here, McCracken is discussing best-selling Latina authors such as Sandra Cisneros whose work, she argues, we can still read as resistant to hegemonic notions of race, gender, and ethnicity. Yet her remark is even more apt in the case of chica lit, which because of its position within the publishing strictures of popular women's genre writing, for the most part must constrain any resistant or subversive "ethnic" or raced commentary to a minimum of quickly suppressed gestures. Thus, subgenres by and about ethnic women and/or women of color, like African American "sistah lit," Indian American "masala lit," and chica lit itself, of necessity contain within themselves often unconscious tensions between niche marketing requirements and the intertwined generic and marketing constraints imposed by the publishing industry. Such constraints assume whiteness as a default norm; the unremarked privileges of whiteness become the foundation for an "add and stir" approach to multicultural inclusion, where "the language of difference . . . is substituted for that of social antagonism. In the attempt to contain ruptural popular movements by winning the struggle for ideological closure, dominant groups soothe over fundamental social contradictions beneath the celebration of diversity" (McCracken 13). McCracken argues, however, that the commodification of what she calls minority texts and authors "is an encoding marked by contradiction," since the text's own "ruptural elements" as well as its relationship with its readers makes for a constantly dynamic rather than static cultural artifact (13–14). Yet delineating a balance between reading chica lit through the lens of the overwhelming ideological weight of what Max Horkheimer and Theodor Adorno called the culture industry's "mass deception" (94), or the dynamic strategies or "ways of operating" of Michel de Certeau's cultural user (xiv) is a delicate and often difficult one. This is especially true of "ethnic" fictions produced *within* an industry as powerful, ideologically and socioeconomically speaking, as the publishers of US popular women's fiction are in the beginnings of the twenty-first century. In reading chica lit in particular, we must remember that these books are produced by authors and consumed by readers who do not (want to) envision themselves as part of a "minority" group. Any possible "ruptural elements" in chica lit are in line with its quick production, hastily though not always easily repressed; yet, the familiarity and comfort of these books' genre conventions help to provide the casual reader the illusion that she has hold of nothing more than a quick and easy read.

PUBLISHING STEREOTYPES

As I have been indicating, any examination of chica lit must pay close attention to the shaping and constraining requirements of plot formulae shared across the rather porous lines of genre fiction. Just as importantly, in looking at chica lit we need to attend to the normative and ideological requirements of mainstream publishing houses, from Harlequin Books to HarperCollins. In fact Latina/o authors and commentators on why Latino writing should be "mainstreamed" make explicit and sometimes invidious comparisons between middle-class Latina/o fiction and the kinds of resistant writing that have come out of now classic Latina/Chicano publishers such as the Bilingual, Floricanto, and Arte Público presses.

A word about presses such as these allows us to understand the context in which chica lit sees itself as correcting "stereotypes" of Latinos. These presses in particular were important not only in shaping a Latino canon but in shaping the kinds of narratives that would gain acceptance, beginning in the early 1970s. In the late 1960s, in the midst of the Chicano Civil Rights *movimiento*, a push for a Chicano cultural nationalist "renaissance" in art, poetry, theater, and fiction motivated small Chicano presses to begin the process of establishing a literary canon. They were looking for works that could serve for what Juan Bruce-Novoa called a "radical expression of a more general threat to the predominant canon. Nationalism has been associated with monolingualism; now the question arises of the polyglot state" (21). Indeed, as he continues, "the emphasis, during the first years of the Chicano Movement . . . on finding any and every text that could be utilized in literature classes, as well as in political consciousness-raising efforts, might lead one to expect that the earliest canons would have been liberally all-inclusive" (133). Yet, as he goes on to argue, the emphasis on a particular idea of (resistant) ethnic identity in fact led to exclusions from these early canons. This was especially true of those like the gay writer John Rechy or the counterculture lawyer "Brown Buffalo" Oscar Zeta Acosta, whose behaviors or sexuality did not fit rapidly solidifying notions about what an authentic Chicano identity looked like: "a claimed and desperately sought-after bond of ethnicity" that overlooked the class and ideological divisions inherent in any large group (137). Particularly important was the establishment, in 1970, of the Quinto Sol press's *el Premio Quinto Sol*, which was awarded once a year for the "best" Chicano novel: "To the satisfaction of some and the continual frustration of others, Anaya, Rivera, and Hinojosa became the Chicano Big Three" in winning this prize (Bruce-Novoa 135). Although much has changed, and changed fundamentally since the 1970s, the popular notion that such canonized texts are all more or less the same in their evocation of an "authentic," working-class, Spanish-speaking, and resistant ethnic identity remains. This perception, especially among younger generations of Chicanos and Latinas, creates a popular illusion of "old school" literary sameness, even if the actuality is quite different.

The difference between a presumably mainstream Latino/a identity, especially since the "Latino explosion" of the 1990s, and that of the oppositional Chicano/Latina old school subject—often marked by poverty, inequity, and oppression—is laid out in a 2013 report on the future of Latino book publishing, written by Examiner.com's Mayra Calvani. In fact, the clarity of the differences makes it worthwhile to look at a couple of extended quotes. Consulting Roberto Cabello, editor and publisher of Floricanto Press, Calvani reports Cabello's belief that "Books written for a Latino audience . . . deal with subjects or address issues that are of special interest to this demographic and must be written in a compelling cultural voice that will strike a chord with Latino readers. . . . the language is often bilingual. The cultural symbols, such as customs, traditions, values and other aspects of social life are Hispanic. . . . 'Every novel becomes an anthropological case study to certain extent, because we are dealing with a different culture, a different group.'" On the other hand, Calvani continues,

> Some [Latino book editors] are weary of stereotypes often depicted in novels, such as the uneducated housewives, the immigrants, the maids, the machista gang members and drug dealers, and the sexy, voluptuous Latinas. According to [former Simon & Schuster editor Marcela Landres, publisher of the e-zine *Latinidad*] . . . "The world does not need another novel written by a college-educated, middle-

class Latino featuring a Latino protagonist who is uneducated and poor," she says. [Leticia Gomez, senior agent at Savvy Literary Services, an agency specializing in Latino books] . . . would like to see these types of characterizations a thing of the past. She believes Latinos are moving up in the world and should be depicted as such. She hopes to see Latinas portrayed as CEOs of their own companies or brilliant nuclear scientists. "On a personal level, I would love to read about a Latino 'James Bond' or 'Bill Gates,'" she says.

These extended quotes simultaneously show a similarity and a stark contrast in the ways publishers of Latino-authored books think about and therefore market *latinidad*, as well as pointing up the problematic nature of both ways of viewing the subject. Both assume that Chicano/Latina fiction must mirror a supposed "truth" about Latinos in general. Yet we cannot view Latinas and Chicanas in the early twenty-first century United States as subjects for anthropological or ethnographical study—this would suggest they are somehow outside the structures of race, gender, and capitalism in the United States, static and to be examined only for their anthropological "culture" and their folkways. Nor, however, can all Latinos or Chicanas "whiten" or accrue sufficient privilege to comfortably imagine themselves in the skin of those most fictive of characters, a "Latino James Bond or Bill Gates."

Puerto Rican cultural critic Frances Negrón-Muntaner theorizes that "*boricua* cultural production is largely made up of the desire to purge, flaunt, deny, destroy and transfigure the constitutive shame of being Puerto Rican from our bodies and public selves" (xiv). Although the vast majority of the chica heroines we will meet here are not Puerto Rican (Valdes's Afro–Puerto Rican Usnavys being the exception), something of the same could be said for most of the chica lit authors I examine here. That is, in their desire to avoid the "stereotypes" of Latinos and, especially, Mexicans and Mexican Americans, a kind of shame is activated that is close to that which Negrón-Muntaner outlines above. This is not the shame she attaches to the ambiguously neocolonial status of Puerto Ricans, but a middle-class Latino/a shame of the "low-class," laboring, poor, heavily accented, and distinctly unfashionable body. As I have noted, chica lit, motivated by this emotion, provides its readers with an instructive, classed correction.

Like white chick lit, chica lit instructs its readers in the obstacles and strivings proper to a professional, heterosexual, and well-educated young woman of the twenty-first century, laying at her feet the fantastic rewards attendant on successfully embodying such a femininity. This kind of instruction is relatively easy; women encounter it—expect and welcome it, even—in every medium and at every turn, from movies to magazines to everyday self-policing. The instructive nature of these fictions becomes more difficult when it must address the question of how a twenty- to thirty-something woman incorporates her unavoidable ethnicity into a recipe for cultural citizenship; that is, how to Americanize her ethnicity by making it commercially viable. From Rios's ethnically confused Marcela to Valdes's self-loathing narrator Lauren to Kathy Cano-Murillo's clueless Star/Estrella, each chica heroine will, at the conclusion of each book, not just understand rationally but *feel* the sense of belonging within the structures of an American late modern capitalism. The salutary lesson here, then, is one that teaches the chica heroine how to fashion "Latinization"; that is, the multiple public and mediated discourses shaping an imagined (pan-) Latino heritage into a rentable commodity—a commodity whose iterable nature is "for rent"—as Arlene Dávila has noted, for a neoliberal vision of a multicultural economy (*Latino Spin* 20).[18] Although there has always been a Latino elite in the United States, Dávila has attributed the relatively recent popular press discovery of a Latino middle class to "the historical hyper-privileging of 'culture' and language as defining elements of Latinidad" (*Latino Spin* 31).

CULTURE AND LATINIZATION

In this book, the terms "Latinization" and "culture" in general refer to the process, on the part of non-Latinos as well as Latinas/os themselves, of imagining, commodifying, and "monetizing" what a Latino cultural heritage looks like in order to fit into a specifically market-oriented, multicultural vision of American cultural citizenship. As we will see, and as Frederick Aldama argues of postethnic fiction, struggles over representation do mean something, for although they may be embodied in fiction or works of art, they have the power for good or for ill to "affect our vision of the world" (109).

Since the 1990s, Latino and Chicana scholars have variously addressed the social and cultural impact on the United States of a growing population of US Latinas and Chicanos, and the rise in the (circular) immigration of Mexicans, Central Americans, South Americans, and Hispanophone Caribbeans. "Latinization" has come to stand as a general term for this complex process. On the one hand, we have the argument that the United States is becoming more and more Latinized: "As a marketer was more than eager to remind me," Dávila writes, "'Everyone wants to be a Hispanic today, people are learning salsa, there's a Hispanicization of American culture, look at the Latin Grammys!'" (*Latino Spin* 9). This is the popular notion, often advanced by proponents of what McCracken has called a "top-down" multiculturalism (*Analyzing World Fiction* 166), that a Latin American ethnicity is in the process of transforming what is popularly assumed to be American culture. On the other hand, Latino scholars have argued for a more nuanced examination of the ways that Latinas and Chicanos are Latinized, or "tropicalized," not just by what hooks calls "white supremacist capitalist patriarchy," but also through their own self-representations as they struggle "to attain power and authority" (Aparicio and Chávez-Silverman 12).[19]

I use the terms Latinization and tropicalization to denote how chica lit and its authors work to imagine what a Latina "culture" looks like, and to show how such a largely imagined culture can be commodified and monetized to provide chica lit characters with American cultural citizenship. Although books like Valdes's can show their readers the diversity of Latin American and Caribbean people, such diversity is still nevertheless ultimately winnowed down into a narrow set of stock images and ideas that then constitute a kind of shorthand signifying "Mexicanness," "Cubanness," "Dominicanness," etc. Here, "culture" is instrumental: that is, it can be used within a framework of American values—patriotism, hard work, the striving for material wealth—as Dávila asserts, "to sell, frame, structure, claim, and reclaim [ethnic] space" (*Barrio Dreams* 9). Indeed, the very notion of "culture" as constituting merely an array of instrumental functions that will make a profit—for example, in New York City's bid to redevelop the Lower East Side as a tourist destination—makes it "especially difficult to grapple with Latinos' differentiation in critical ways" (*Latino Spin* 9).

Genre and its conventions are the most important shaping and constraining elements in chica lit. These are in turn inextricably tied to the commercialization of popular women's fiction. In the first chapter of this book, I examine the ways chica lit's representations of Latinas are part of larger marketing assumptions about ethnicity and Americanization. I advance the argument that chica lit is indebted especially to romance and to chick lit, showing how the elements of these genres function for chica lit's particular corrective and prescriptive needs. I also argue here that because of its portrayal of a gendered ethnicity and race, chica lit also avails itself of elements belonging to other categories: career girl fiction, paranormal romance, and ethnic coming-of-age novels. My second chapter shows how an investment in the concept of a "culture of poverty" functions to shape certain chica lit characters as foils for the necessary ascent of the chica heroine to a middle-class life. Here, questions of poverty lead directly into a discussion of the ways class is reframed in these novels as style and taste, which, notwithstanding their presumably private nature, also work to reinforce material and social hierarchies. In particular, the use of kitsch as personal style and domestic décor aids Mexican American fiction in warding off intimations of danger conjured by imaginings of a Mexico infested with poverty and illicit drug gangs.

My third chapter looks at the ways both Latina authors and their work are shaped for a niche market through a process of "Latinization" that transforms potentially threatening ethnic heritage into products for consumption and profit. Here, authors engage in vexed conversations about their relationship to an ambiguously imagined *latinidad* and to the Spanish language itself, while the necessity for a cultural Americanization of their characters is played out in prescriptions for how to leverage "culture," here most often imagined as food, into romance and careers. My fourth and final chapter investigates Alisa Valdes's *Dirty Girls on Top* and Lisa Wixon's *Dirty Blonde and Half Cuban*, where, unusually, characters move outside the boundaries of the United States. Here I investigate the seemingly logical solution to the chica lit heroine's identity crisis, which would be to visit their countries of origin. I show the ways Valdes's narrative strategies work to recontain the excessive nature of a dirty and dangerous Mexico, at the same time that Wixon's story attempts to reframe US images of Cuba within the constraints of romance conventions.

Chapter 1

Genre and the Romance Industry

As I have noted, the formulae of women's genre fiction—that is, the accepted and, most importantly, familiar plot patterns and conventions—particularly of the romance novel and contemporary chick lit, act as processes or "doings," as Frederick Aldama and Ramón Saldívar note, for constructing as well as working through answers to questions about women's cultural and economic options.[1] Yet the delineations of specific genres are always blurred, as scholars of popular genre such as Catherine Gledhill attest: they are "not discrete systems, consisting of a fixed number of listable items" (64). As we will see, the formulaic boundaries of chica lit are shared by, though its narrative concerns are also constrained by, those of contemporary romance, paranormal romance, chick lit, and career girl fiction. In fact, I argue that chica lit's unusual (for popular women's fiction) set of questions makes it necessary for its authors to choose from all of these plot conventions the elements that will best address such concerns. At the same time, I argue, these elements also impose constraints on chica lit's overtly stated concerns with ethnicity and Americanization, as well as with the undeniable facets of Latino and Chicano poverty and a growing US anti-immigration sentiment. It is quite possible to work creatively and even brilliantly within a form's constraints. Established writers may feel freer to experiment within the bounds of these forms but the more lucrative the romance and chick lit market, the more formulaic the writing tends to be, and the greater the emphasis is on new and up-and-coming authors to conform. And romance and chick lit publishing, including all the niche imprints and presses belonging to large houses, is very lucrative indeed. The Romance Writers of America (RWA), a nonprofit trade association, estimates from BookStats that by 2013 romance novels—a wide and encompassing category—sold 1.8 billion dollars' worth of books ("Romance Industry Statistics"). Indeed, despite the assumption of new freedoms for writing and publishing opened up by the internet, these genre boundaries still constitute part of what is required by editors, publishing corporations, and retailers. And despite the growth of niche markets for African American romance and ethnic chick lit, we find upon closer examination that the nearer these books hew to strict genre elements, the more the narrative must struggle with the contradictory positions of its racially or ethnically marked heroines. In other words, the tools of popular genre cannot completely provide the narrative logic for putting ethnic women's bodies center stage.

Chica lit is different from white romance and chick lit in its use of Latina characters, as well as its sometimes overtly didactic nature. Yet because the genre conventions and publishing requirements of contemporary romance novels have provided a template for both chick and chica lit, it is helpful to look at the ways in which such a template functions, especially now, in the context of early twenty-first-century US corporate publishing. This chapter examines, first, the genre outlines of contemporary romance fiction and its relationship to chick and chica lit. Next, I continue my argument that genre formulae now work in a feedback loop with the requirements of mass marketing. We will see how romance and chick lit, and by extension, chica lit, are by their very nature as genre writing, embedded both within the exigencies for successful sales and within the cultural logic, already discussed above, of current US economic policies and practices.

Besides chica lit, Mary Castillo and Lara Rios have also written Latina romances, or have had their chica lit books published by presses that specialize in romance fiction. The publisher of the e-zine *Latinidad*, Marcela Landres, offers interviews, advice, and tips for Latina/o authors looking to get published, especially by a large company. In her September 2, 2006, edition Landres gave this advice to Latina authors: "I often advise writers to think of themselves as small business owners and their manuscripts as the product or service they sell. Mary Castillo took this concept one step further by composing a business plan for her writing career" ("Business Plan"). Landres then features a brief interview with Castillo, in which she asks readers, "Have you ever had an agent or editor who was not Latino tell you that the characters in your manuscript weren't 'Latino enough'? If so, you're not alone. Mary Castillo didn't let that stop her, and her persistence paid off in not one, but two book deals. Note that Mary met one of her editors at the RWA's National Convention. Further proof that writing conferences can be worth the price of admission" ("Q&A: Mary Castillo"). The interview continues as Castillo discusses her experiences trying to get her first chica lit fiction published: "I walked into the Publisher Spotlight session for Avon Romance at RWA's National Convention in New York, determined to take one more chance to find a home for Tamara. . . . So for those writers out there who are banging their heads against the walls because you don't have a chola, a hoochie mama, a barefoot peasant, or a mystical all-knowing abuelita in your story (I'm being facetious!), there are publishers and agents looking for fresh and contemporary Latina stories" ("Q&A"). Besides the (seemingly requisite) rejection of "old school" Latina/o "stereotypes," a large part of chica lit's success, then, is found in the fact that its business side is rooted—in terms of genre as well as in market terms—in contemporary romance. Yet romance novels themselves have morphed over the last couple of decades. Wendell and Tan in their *Beyond Heaving Bosoms* delineate between "Old Skool" and "New Skool" romance novels. "Old Skool" are the kind we typically associate with giant romance publishers such as Harlequin (sometimes used as a kind of generic reference to all romances of a certain basic type). The Old Skool romance, pared down, according to Wendell and Tan, looks like this:

> Boy meets girl.
> Holy crap, shit happens!
> Eventually, the boy gets the girl back.
> They live Happily Ever After. (11)

As Wendell and Tan note, this formula is "deceptively simple" (11). Indeed, Pamela Regis notes in her *A Natural History of the Romance Novel* that the romance is "old, flexible," and still ill-defined (7), although her work does attempt to define it: "The romance novel is a work of prose fiction that tells the story of the courtship and betrothal of one or more heroines" (14), and proceeds to enumerate its eight narrative elements. As she continues, she presents us with a pocket history of eighteenth- and nineteenth-century changes in women's status that effected changes in the romance: "We found three sweeping society trends—affective individualism (acting for one's own happiness), property rights for women, and . . . marrying for love . . . that informed, propelled, and inspired the courtships" (108). Writing in 2000, Regis averred that in romance, these three motivations for courtship were already in place; now at the beginning of the US twenty-first century, these "books present portraits of women in command of their lives" (110). Regis's contention that in the requisite happy ending "the heroine is freed [by overcoming the element of the barrier to love] and the reader rejoices" does not tell us why marriage or romantic love, rather than some other triumph, must be the end result of this process. Nor do all contemporary romance (or chick lit, or chica lit) women characters begin the narrative as "being in command of their lives." Indeed, chica lit imbues the twenty-first-century romance's concerns with discourses of "affective individualism" and the question of women's property. In chica lit, these are translated into a neoliberal belief in the heroine's individual power (sometimes helped by girlfriend power) to solve the seemingly private problems of her life—how to be a Latina in the United States, how to be a "modern" woman, how to have time for a career and a romance—and made even more complex by uncertainties about contemporary access to the means of property, here transformed into worries about work and careers.

Thus the road to rejoicing that Regis's readers follow in the romance novel is often a rockier one both for chick lit and chica lit, although each chica lit novel faithfully if with difficulty brings its readers the requisite happy ending. In fact, the journey to that happy ending can be so fraught with problems that scholars of women's genre writing have begun to argue that the immensely popular and influential subgenre of chick lit, like the inheritors of *Bridget Jones's Diary*, are, in their representations of the advice and admonitions surrounding women, actually novels of parody and disenchantment. Leah Guenther asserts in her discussion of chick lit that its characters "struggle with conflicting social messages that compel them simultaneously to find a man, be independent, build a career, start a family, have sex indiscriminately and be chaste" (86).[2]

At the same time, like chick lit and contemporary romance, chica lit often exhibits a frothy style, accompanied by enticing descriptions of luxury items and beautiful homes. Despite these novels' recourse to seductive scenes of luxury and ease, however, scholars like Suzanne Ferriss and Tania Modleski maintain that chick lit responds to actual social and financial fears and anxieties of young women at the turn of the century. Yet the idea that chick lit and romance fiction "respond" to their readers' realities, or the claim that they "mirror" their audiences' lives, is, especially in the case of chica lit, misleading. As we will see, these novels are written in such a way as to make their characters and situations "relatable" to the reader. In this way, what Regis calls "barriers" to women's happiness are indeed set up in these fictional stories as they are in real life. However, as she notes, such barriers and conflicts only exist to be overcome; indeed they must be overcome if the reader is to be satisfied in her demand for a happy ending (15). If chica lit does, as I argue here, have its roots in popular women's genres like romance and chick lit, then like in those genres the characters in chica lit will face conflicts, barriers, and even disillusionments. For chica lit, however, the impulse to a "corrective" narrative, wherein it is (with some narrative difficulty) demonstrated that Latinas can indeed be middle-class Americans, shapes the narrative into an instructive one. Here chica lit joins up once again with the generic goal of romance and chick lit to reassure both character and reader that in spite of many obstacles, those who learn proper (feminine as well as ethnic) behavior will indeed experience freedom and rejoicing. Particularly in chica lit, then, instructions for how Latinas can leverage their ethnicity into successful Americanization mirror, not so much their audience, but other romance and chick lit narratives as advice manuals, which show women how to behave in ways that tend to benefit the established social order of things.

If this is so, then chica lit's origins in romance and in chick lit call for characters who will finally, through lessons learned and rewards earned, accept the neoliberal reshapings of their socioeconomic world. Yet chica lit must perform the extra step of reframing its generic connections to other popular women's writing in order to accommodate Latina characters who are in real-world material terms less likely to wind up with successful, middle-class lives.

Shifting economic policies that tend to privilege privatization over government and state regulations and safety nets require a new set of economic relations between workers and employers. Although she is writing about paranormal romance, Erin Young argues that "the conventional romance narratives of the 1980s and prior reflect romantic relationships in the context of Fordist capitalism. The paranormal romance subgenre that emerges in the 1990s, on the other hand, explores the changing constructions of male and female subjectivity under flexible accumulation" (205–6). This insight may help illuminate the place chica lit occupies in relationship to its "disillusions." Following David Harvey's analysis of cultural changes in postmodernity, Erin Young defines flexible accumulation as the kind of labor that "marks the transition from mass production to small-scale production, the rise of the service industry, and the growth of 'flexible' employment arrangements (in terms of hours, contracts, work locations, etc.)" (205). Young argues that the instability of such arrangements, and the social changes they require, can give rise to "new configurations of gender roles and gender relations," especially in the paranormal werewolf romances she examines.

Yet in paranormal as well as in "realistic" chica lit, such disillusionment and fiscal instability is not allowed to refigure gender roles; instead, these roles are reframed as a set of problems to be overcome specifically through the heroine's working life, and which in the overcoming will also show our chica heroine the proper ways to leverage her ethnicity into a culturally American access to material well-being.

Chica lit thus functions, as I have been arguing, as behavior manual and advice column for the Latina's engagement with those changing socioeconomic structures to which Young and Harvey refer, in her vexed search for what Alisa Valdes has called a "Latino American biculturalism" (*Lauren's Saints* np). Castillo's *Switchcraft*, Kathy Cano-Murillo's *Waking Up*, Rios's *Becoming Latina*, and Acosta's *Cocktails at Casa Dracula* series all provide examples of how chica lit borrows from career girl, paranormal, and coming-of-age narratives in order to map a "path to [assimilated, American] adulthood" for the didactic purpose of suggesting proper behaviors for romantic and material success in a (bi)cultural US citizenship.

For example, *Switchcraft*'s use of the omniscient narrator allows us to recognize, early on, that an accidental, paranormal body-switching will point its characters on the path to a self-understanding that includes material success for both main characters. As we meet the main character Aggie, her illusions about her carefree and materially successful life are already being shattered at the beginning of the book. Because she's not married, still rents, and has a failing business, Aggie "felt so childish" next to her best friend Nely's husband, house, and baby; Nely "seemed so . . . so grown up." On the other hand, Nely herself feels fat, "heavy-footed and slatternly" in the presence of Aggie's well-toned, child-free, "high maintenance" life (11, 14). Clearly, both women will be learning lessons, which result in their partnering in Aggie's business: one about how to grow up and be a responsible businesswoman and wife, the other about how to value what she has while parlaying her skills as a mother into managing a thriving business. Meanwhile, *Cocktails at Casa Dracula*'s Milagro will learn that her prestigious degree will not land her a job, and subsequently she must encounter and overcome the fact that because she is Mexican American, her love of gardening may be perceived as merely the "natural" desire of a Mexican laborer; it is, finally, her feisty Mexican American temperament, coupled with her paranormal adventures, that provide her with a path to true adult self-understanding. Problems persist and the road to assimilation must be mapped out even without paranormal help; Marcela of *Becoming Latina* is shattered by news that the Mexican father she's loved all her life is not her biological father, who it turns out is white. The nature of such disappointments are, as we shall see, specific to Latinas at the turn of the twenty-first century:

though the characters are imagined, they must face real-world problems: access to education, barriers to material well-being, the maintenance of coupledom in uneasy financial and cultural circumstances.

At the same time, both disillusionment and its attendant problems and conflicts are also demanded by the generic armature of a long history of sentimental, romantic, and chick lit. For centuries, the popular women's novel has presented characters who must overcome barriers to happiness. For the contemporary chica lit novels' intended mode of reading—that is, superficial—such a framework is often familiar enough to the reader to help to paper over glaring contradictions, which really *would* be disillusioning. Instead, it is the required resolution of such conflicts—and even the "dissing" of illusions—that furthers the positive nature of chica lit's underlying didactic mission, so that heroine and reader can derive the reward they deserve for learning their lessons, and follow the path to understanding themselves as grown-up, twenty-first-century cultural Americans. This resolution is the happy ending.

Even in those chica lit novels that voice muffled protests against structural inequality, endings are especially important. Radway discusses the importance of endings to women's romance reading strategies by noting how many women in her study told her that before buying the book, they always paged to the back first to make sure the novel concluded properly. Radway noted that her romance readers chose "their romances carefully [reading the end first, for example] in an attempt to assure themselves of a reading experience that will make them feel happy and hold out the promise of utopian bliss, a state they willingly acknowledge to be rare in the real world but one, nevertheless, that they do not want to relinquish *as a conceptual possibility*" (100). Endings must give the reader that "conceptual possibility" that Radway acknowledges is part of the "romantic myth" (200). It is important to understand that in the chica lit novel, however, such seemingly mythic utopian bliss is written not as fantasy but as *possibility*. That actual ending, the reader knows, may not happen to her but it is always *possible* that romance and material well-being might be hers; this is particularly true with chica lit's didactic map-making strategies. This element of possibility is why it is important to understand that, as Radway notes, readers also expect complexity and "reality" in their novels: "the novelistic character is intended to appear as a complex, human figure whose often contradictory traits and motives are a function of the need to deal . . . with an entirely contingent and particular reality that is . . . unpredictable as well" (200). In chica lit, material success is represented as opening the way to a certain kind of unpredictable possibility. In the happy ending, its characters finally now inhabit a world of more "personal choices," particularly import-ant for Latinas. In this way, chica lit gestures toward both the con-tingent and particular realities of "being Latina" in the United States even in its presumably "fantasy" plots and endings. Poverty, or the specter of it, is presented as the other side of accomplishment, and thus as rigidly predictable and closed. The material uncertainties and even chaotic lives often called forth in belonging to a generally dis-enfranchised group of people must be, once raised as problems at the beginning of each book, negotiated into a harmonious but apparently possible as well as open-ended order, through the romantic and chick lit convention of the "happy ending" opening the characters' lives to options. Of course, not all options are on the table; indeed, as Acosta noted in a personal communication, "In my first version of my first book, Milagro tells the men pursuing her, 'If you ever grow up, give me a call,' and she walks out the door. My agent said that she couldn't sell the book if it didn't have a 'happy ending.' I told her that a young woman standing on her own two feet *was* a happy ending. Evidently, my idea of a happy ending is not the universal definition, so I had to change the end to get the book deal" (e-mail message to author, Janu-ary 19, 2014).

As different as each situation may seem, endings must show how each character has learned those lessons necessary to point her on the way to a reordering of romantic, professional, and ethnic identities. Each chica must be, if not completely fulfilled (for example she might not yet be married), content with her journey toward her growth as a culturally enfranchised American. The iteration of such endings accustoms readers to a narrative that leads its characters to an opening-out—not into the unknowable but into what has already been envi-sioned by the book as a place where characters (and by extension read-ers) know who they are or at least who they are becoming. Despite the illusion of open-endedness, these endings are actually comfortable in that they point to places that themselves appear to be surrounded by the glow of real fulfillment. Thus even the seemingly bleak and un-chica-lit-like introduction to Valdes's third, self-published *Dirty Girls*, while unusual, should not fill the accomplished reader of genre fiction with too much alarm about its ending. Referring to "the economic realities of our time," Valdes writes, "I, like so many of us, have watched the economy of the United States plummet into recession. . . . I have seen many of my friends lose jobs and homes, with little hope of ever recovering, thanks to a banking industry and federal government that have been corrupted almost beyond repair" (*Lauren's Saints* np). Nowhere in her brief meditation on such economic realities, however, is there a sense that the economic troubles of the Great Recession might have any other cause than an unexplained sense of "corruption." Such might seem like a disturbing loose end if this somber message were not swiftly undercut by her assertion on the same page that in the midst of such downbeat "realism," readers will still be treated to Valdes's "own signature . . . [a] relatable American Latino biculturalism and sizzling hot romance" (np). So, despite rape, a murderous stalker, a child born with autism, the loss of a husband and a job, problems with bulimia and alcoholism and marriages, this book's ending again highlights lessons learned and happiness earned. By the end of this book Lauren is madly in love with the (now, in the real world, infamous) hot cowboy John, who has just killed her murdering stalker. Rebecca, the mother of the autistic child, is in counseling with her husband André but asserts that things will work out fine (she just has to learn to separate André, psychologically, from her father), and Usnavys has made friends with her enemy Taina and plans to become successful again by promoting Taina's beauty salon through contacts with Usnavys's wealthy and famous *sucias*. Indeed, on the ultimate page of the book Valdes rewards the reader for sticking with it by pointing her forward to Amazon.com, where she can "purchase the X-rated Very Dirty Chapter," which describes Lauren and John's first sexual encounter. She also promises that if the reader wants to "find out what happens with Usnavys and Rebecca next, be on the lookout for two new Dirty Girls novels in the next year" (np).[3]

CLASS WITHOUT MONEY

Stephanie Harzewski emphasizes that historically, popular women's writing has deep "consumer roots" in the family tree of women's writing. These roots, she argues, connect earlier women's writing to a late twentieth- and early twenty-first-century conflation of consumer and personal identity in chick lit (43). As Harzewski continues, chick lit often "revisits the 'class without money' conflict that pervades the novel of manners tradition . . . [and] domestic fiction's marriage plot, chronicling the heroines' fortune on the marriage market and assessing contemporary courtship behavior, dress, and social motives" (41). Plots have long histories, true; yet as Andrew Uzendoski notes, such an undertaking offers "limited insight into the cultural and historical context" of subgenres such as chick or chica lit: "we must read [these novels] through an apparatus that attends to contemporary consumer practices" (10). His suggestion helps us think about chica lit itself as part of an apparatus of thought that includes the ways in which domesticity's by now seemingly inherent entanglement with consumer culture has, since the aftermath of the Second World War, increasingly conflated femininity with consumption. Employing this idea, I take into consideration the romance industry's vast web of marketing tools, examining how such tools shape both the narratives themselves and their reception. Publishers, authors, and readers alike have been able to take up, and expand on, these tools—often author- and reader-dependent—as well as romance presses' savvy use of the internet and marketing tie-ins. Romance readers already had well-connected reading communities—for example, newsletters sent through the mail to subscribers have been around for more than twenty years. In this way, the publishing especially of women's popular writing such as chica lit has been able to take advantage of similar ways to construct reading communities online: review blogs, author blogs, author interviews, e-books through Kindle or other devices, apps for reading on smartphones.

Because these fictions are articulated on the skeleton of the contemporary woman's romance formula, it helps to understand the logic that underlies the success of contemporary romance fictions, as well as their seemingly relentless juggernaut marketing engines. Thus, for example, the proliferation of more and more niche-specific series by large romance publishing firms such as Harlequin, with accompanying instructions, writing guidelines, and even blogs with publisher tips (available on their website) for, at last count, thirty-three different series, from their relatively new "Harlequin Digital First" to the strangely compelling "Harlequin Medical Romance." Despite the seeming differences among these series, Harlequin's how-to guide seems to apply to each of them: "Know and respect your readers—choose the most recent novels and read widely across the romance market. Then target the series/genre that excites you and suits your voice" ("How to Write"). Although it may seem like only common sense, this "tip" makes it clear that aspiring writers must at least try to identify a niche (the "series/genre") to whose editors they are likely to sell their books, as well as understand the cues and conventions of their wide reading "across the romance market." Harlequin's vast marketing network also encourages web connectivity with blogs for every series, short promotional videos for specific book titles or series, interviews with authors, Harlequin.com social networking sites, and a "So You Think You Can Write" contest, with a book contract as first prize (Harlequin.com). As we have seen, the American Association of Romance Writers, an umbrella organization for publishers as well as writers, holds yearly conventions as well, where prospective authors can get information and "network" with prospective publishers.

While genre boundaries are increasingly porous, chick lit and romance fictions, for example, have become more and more niche-oriented. This can lead to some confusion as to which kinds of fiction are marketed as what, and why. As I briefly noted in my introduction, "chica lit" is not a term that publishing houses use. Nevertheless, gatekeepers and others within the publishing industry have certain expectations for popular Latina fiction. "Before the book was sold, my first agent asked me to include more Spanish words and phrases, and to remove terms in French and German. After the sale, my editor wanted me to include more descriptions of clothes and parties and to delete some political commentary. I was suddenly termed a writer of 'women's fiction,' rather than a writer. I expressed my objections, including my dislike of the cover art with the girl in the red-ruffled dress, hoop earrings, and high heels, but I had to compromise to get in the door" (Acosta np). Acosta accepts this compromise as well as the fact that she is regularly pigeonholed as a Latina writer. "I have no problem with accepting the inevitability of being categorized, and then subverting expectations."

Macmillan/St. Martin's, which has published six of Alisa Valdes's chica lit novels, simply lists them, without a label, under its Griffin imprint, which publishes a wide range of fiction and nonfiction. Those books by Berta Platas that have been identified in the popular press and on websites as "chica lit"—*Cinderella Lopez* and *Lucky Chica*—have also been published (without labels) by St. Martin's. On the other hand, her "Latina romance" novels such *Miami Heat* and *To Catch a Dream* are published by Pinnacle's Encanto imprint as well as by the romance super-publisher Kensington. Lara Rios's chica lit novels were published (without a generic label) by Berkley, an imprint of Penguin. Rios, however, also writes popular women's fiction under the name Julia Amante for the romance press Hachette, including the recent *Evenings at the Argentine Club* and *Say You'll Be Mine*, both of which, it seems, could just as easily qualify for the appellation of chica lit.

Online marketing and discussion of chica lit relies mostly on authors' blogs and interviews as well as posts and reviews in readers' blogs directed more generally toward women's fiction, especially romance and chick lit. Specific information about the writing and publishing of chica lit is spread throughout the web: calls for chica lit writing contests, writing conferences, and writing workshops are often to be found on authors' blogs and websites. Kathy Cano-Murillo even conducts a Crafty Chica Cruise every year, although her blog informs us that 2013 was the last year of the cruise. The internet itself, and its marketing tie-ins and spinoffs, means of course that at the beginning of the twenty-first century, the economics of publishing books have shifted.

In examining these shifts more closely, we have to start with Valdes. Valdes has been engaged from the start in the vast arena of book- and self-promotions, online presence, and product tie-ins. In addition to maintaining film and television rights to her books, self-publishing several of her books, and producing a faux blog by a (faux) Latina actress, early on she teamed up with the website PartyLaunch.com to sponsor her books via Tupperware-style promotional parties. According to this company's website, Valdes "used her own web site, her blog, a clever contest, pre-launch interviews and more. . . . some of the parties featured fun, cosmo-sipping, 'Sex and the City' themes" (PartyLaunch 2009). For her sequel *Dirty Girls on Top*, of 2009, book parties automatically entered guests to win "a trip to the Fairmont Princess Resort to have lunch with Alisa." These prizes were sponsored by Southwest Airlines, *People en Español*, and Barnes and Noble (PartyLaunch 2009).[4]

Publishers themselves have had to run just to keep up with the ever-morphing ways the internet has grown, ultimately learning to use it to lure in prospective readers. Not so long ago, those writers whose work had been rejected by one of the recognized presses such as Harlequin or Hachette often turned to publishing their work online. The makers of e-readers, especially Amazon, found very quickly that such platforms (and their cross-platform applications) could offer a place where writers' self-published works could go straight to an online format, from mini-"chapters" to novellas to full books; not lagging far behind, presses themselves realized they could offer imprints and series devoted entirely to e-books.[5]

The pace of publishing in romance, chick lit, and chica lit particularly makes these works seem more disposable—more commodified, more consumable—than, say, the initial newspaper serialization of Charles Dickens's novels. As Irin Carmon tells us in her article "Romance Novels Are Steaming up E-reader Screens," more and more authors of women's genres—in particular, the romance—see themselves not just as writers but, perforce, as businesswomen:

> It's a new world, and the women who read, write, and edit romances are blazing the trail into it. Authors' careers may increasingly look like that of Trish Milburn, a writer who . . . has what she calls a "three-pronged attack": She has published four books in print with Harlequin and is contracted to do three more. She has written young-adult paranormal books for a small Southern press, and last spring, she self-published a women's-fiction novel about a mother-daughter relationship. Would she be interested in writing for Carina [a new e-romance series from Harlequin]? "I don't say no to any possibility," she says. "It's all part of a bigger business plan. I don't like to have all my eggs in one basket." (113)

And as Lara Rios, (interviewed under her Latina romance pen name Julia Amante) bravely notes, "Marketing can be fun, but it can also consume a lot of your writing time. Authors have to understand that writing a book is only the first step. Then comes letting the world know about the great book you've written. This involves a lot of self-promotion. This can be done with blogs, social media, making personal appearances, being part of writer's groups, going to conferences where readers are" ("Julia Amante"). Nor, as Carmon goes on, does the possibility of pirating e-books seem to be of much concern to authors or publishers. In fact, Carina romance e-books are published without digital rights management (DRM), a technology embedded in electronic media like e-books that prevents the user from sharing it with other users: "readers chafe at [DRM]. On AllRomance.com, DRM titles comprise half of inventory but only 4% of sales in 2010, says chief operating officer Lori James. . . . 'Our theory is that it doesn't prevent piracy because any pirate can strip DRM in about 30 seconds,' says James. 'DRM instead inhibits casual sharing, an important part of the reading process and the purchasing process'" (114). As Radway has noted about the importance of the very act of reading for women (reading romances, in the case of her study), "the simple event of picking up a book enabled them to deal with the particular pressures and tensions encountered in their daily round of activities" (87). This increased ability to deal with the pressures of their everyday lives included, as she maintains, the sense of being part of a community of (women) readers. The importance of a reading community whose members share books, likes and dislikes, reviews, and recommendations—whether formally through a newsletter or a regular blog, or more informally between a few friends—cannot be overstated when it comes to women's popular books. This is especially true for those categories clustered around romance-inflected books (in whatever guise—bodice-ripper, chick lit, chica lit), with their ever-changing niche markets coupled with a core of comfortingly stable generic formulae. In this world, the production and consumption of women's popular fictions happen at an astounding rate. Two friends sharing a book may lose the publisher a sale or two, but the press is almost guaranteed to gain sales when those two recommend the book to others. If genres like chica lit are inextricably intertwined with generic formulae like those of the romance, the comforting formulae and communal reading aspects of the romance and chick lit as well as chica lit are now bound up with consumer culture in self-reflexive ways.

COMING-OF-AGE CHICAS

A few scholars have noted that chick lit (and by extension chica lit) contain elements of the coming-of-age novel. Stephanie Harzewski, musing on the commercial nature of (white) chick lit, notes that "Ultimately, the phenomenon of *Sex and the City*, and chick lit's commercial success, leaves the feminist scholar to ponder the degree to which a female *bildungsroman* with a heterosexual protagonist can dissociate itself from the marriage plot, and the marriage plot from the pleasures of acquisition" (*Chick Lit* 122). Looking at the ethnic bildungsroman can help to illuminate the ways chica lit's market orientation as popular contemporary (ethnic) romance borrows questions of ethnicity and assimilation from the more radical Chicana coming-of-age novel, and how in the borrowing such concerns have shifted. In the United States, the coming of age novel has been and continues to be a favored genre for ethnic authors since the first decades of the twentieth century. Ethnic coming-of-age novels have often represented, and attempted to negotiate, the tensions inherent in an Americanization that demands the ethnic person's abandonment of links to the "old country" as a necessity for inclusion and participation in US citizenship and society. They have also worked as imaginative documents of how young ethnic people could move away from repressive, old ideas and values and into the new, seemingly limitless freedom of becoming American.

If we are to look to the motivations and restrictions of genre in our analysis of gender and race in chica lit, we find that the coming-of-age genre constitutes significant influences on both chick and chica lit. The combination of genres that make up chick and chica lit has, among other things, also resulted in a small explosion of South Asian American lit (or "masala lit") about young, upwardly mobile South Asian American women. Critical reception of masala lit helps to understand some of the same ideological pressures, especially in terms of Americanization, present in chica lit. Pamela Butler and Jigna Desai maintain in their study of South Asian American lit that in "women of color subgenres such as Chica Lit and Sistah Lit . . . the characters' engagements with femininity and gender are often articulated through questions of race, nation, ethnicity, and socioeconomic class" (Butler and Desai 4). It is important to remember, as they point out, that the formulaic nature of chick lit itself shapes how these issues will look to the reader. Butler and Desai maintain that "white chick lit" does duty as bildungsroman as well, in that these novels "describe the coming of age of the modern subject and narrate the integration of the citizen-subject into the nation-state. . . . More specifically, the *bildungsroman* traces the development and coming into maturation of the individual as she finds her proper location in community and society. . . . In modern *bildungsromans*, this maturation is increasingly marked as the ability to adapt oneself to a globalized society, to gain entrance into a professional labor class and to access its corresponding bourgeois luxury and leisure consumption" (15).

If this is the case, then, chica lit also enfolds aspects of its sister genre, the Chicana coming-of-age narrative. The Chicana coming-of-age story itself appeared first in the mid-1970s; Annie Eysturoy, in her *Daughters of Self-Creation*, maintains that the 1976 "*Victuum* by Isabella Ríos is the first *Bildungsroman* to be published by a Chicana" (33). Yet if the genres of chica lit and Chicana bildungsroman are related, they are also deeply estranged; when we look at chica lit's appropriation of the Chicana bildungsroman, an ideological doubling-back of sorts takes place. That is, because Chicana coming-of-age novels have both emerged from, as well as critiqued, the discourses of the Chicano *movimiento* of the mid-1960s through the 1970s, they themselves reshaped the masculine ethnic bildungsroman by articulating a Chicano discourse of ethnic rights, enfranchisement, and authenticity while also demanding a Chicana gendered autonomy in ethnic and mainstream cultural spaces. Particularly in the years during and after the height of Black and Chicano nationalism, many of these stories now acknowledged that brown and black people, by reason of their inability to become fully white, might always have difficulty in gaining full enfranchisement. As Eysturoy puts it, "During the twentieth century . . . the process of development has been increasingly characterized by disillusionment and confrontation with a hostile environment . . . uncertainties of contemporary life are often reflected in the often indeterminate endings. . . . in which social integration is only obtained through some kind of compromise" (10). In this sense, chica lit's close ties to the concerns of romance and chick lit—class, consumer capital, and (heterosexual) romance—often clash with any engagement with questions of resistant ethnicity. Instead, chica lit effects something of a return to an assimilationist model of the bildungsroman, one that is concerned only with the acculturation of the ethnic character into a successful American subject.

US fiction about immigration and ethnicity has long narrativized both individual success and American enfranchisement through the coming-of-age genre. The generic assumptions of this model of the bildungsroman, as Jeffrey Sammons notes, still have "something to do with *Bildung*, that is, with the early bourgeois, humanistic concept of the shaping of the individual self . . . through acculturation . . . to the threshold of maturity" (41).[6] Many chica lit novels' beginnings signal that the character's journey must be upward, toward an acculturated adulthood. Aggie of *Switchcraft* longs to be an adult; Star of *Waking Up* still lives with her parents; Milagro of *Happy Hour at Casa Dracula* has issues with her mother and lives in a rented basement apartment; Lauren in *Dirty Girls* has issues with her Cuban father, causing her therapist to tell her she needs a "Cubadectomy." Yet most importantly, especially for Latinos and Chicanas, mainstream Latino bildungsromans serve a social as well as political function: to follow the young, often second-generation Latino character's journey to adulthood as it maps a journey of assimilation, citizenship, and eventual mainstream success. That is, the youthful second (or even third or fourth) generation can stand in, via synecdoche, for an entire "ethnic" group, while the character's coming of age into adulthood can stand in for the group's maturation into fully enfranchised and American consumers. In some important ways, chica lit gestures toward this safer and often more conservative trajectory of ethnic youth growing to American maturity. Indeed, chica lit authors have written assimilative young adult bildungsromans as well, thus separating themselves from the 1970s and '80s turn toward a Chicana model that demanded American recognition of plurality rather than assimilation.

Finally, another development, around the midpoint of the twentieth century, enabled women writers to write fiction that negotiated the growing necessity in the United States for white, middle-class women to have jobs, often even after marriage. As the women's movement increasingly demanded that professions open for women, ethnic women—who often still had to work—might be able to imagine that their daughters could become professionals. The rising popularity of romance novels where the woman might hold a meaningful job, could by the turn of the century combine with the astounding popularity of chick lit characters who had, if not careers, at least steady jobs (even if, like Bridget of *Bridget Jones's Diary* or Lauren of *Dirty Girls Social Club*, they might hate such jobs). Such possibilities—however slim in real life—opened the door for Latina authors to imagine cultural assimilation at least in part through the heroine's own attainment of material well-being.

SEX AND THE CAREER CHICA

In 1962 Helen Gurley Brown asserted in her *Sex and the Single Girl* that the single "career girl" is "the newest glamour girl of our times." This bromide often seems to be as casually embraced, even in chica lit, as it was some fifty years ago. At the same time, women's disenchantment with the still largely masculine-oriented structures of many workplaces has led to depictions of chica heroines whose jobs, and lives, are less than glamorous. In addition, Latina characters must face the largely unspoken fact that in real life, Latinas and Chicanas have less opportunity for entrance into well-paying professional careers than do white women. Thus, we must ask ourselves how working (or having a career) functions in chica lit. In her discussion of "career girl" precedents to chick lit, Harzewski notes, "A harbinger of the sexual revolution and figurative how-to guide to the best of everything, [former editor of *Cosmopolitan*] Helen Gurley Brown's *Sex and the Single Girl* (1962) stands, in title and spirit, as a foundational predecessor to the chick lit genre. . . . [I]ts rejection of the cultural myth that every girl must be married and its directives for having a fulfilling and romantic, if not enviable, life as a single woman underlie chick lit" (141). Although I would argue that neither chick nor chica lit reject "the cultural myth that every girl must be married," the "directive" that young women who wish to be glamorous must have careers lies at the heart of chica lit's didactic drive toward cultural Americanization as well. Having the means to consume no longer assumes that a woman will be supported (at least entirely) by a man; and for chica lit having a job, or better yet a career or profession, is of central importance in recouping Latinas as middle-class citizens.

Not all chica lit, of course, represents paid work in the same ways. In the novels I examine, issues of work fall into two broad groups. The first group includes the writings of Valdes and Rios as well as Mary Castillo's *Switchcraft*: in these, the oft-mentioned assertion that the chica heroine has a career fills in for the lack of scenes of actual work. These novels follow the lead of contemporary women's popular fiction: Who remembers seeing any of the four girlfriends of *Sex and the City* actually toiling at their various jobs? Such scenes would work as "downers" for that element of enjoyment these narratives must employ. Yet for chica lit the assertion that each character has already achieved—or soon, it is promised, will achieve—a successful career carries much more weight, acting, as I have been emphasizing, not as fantasy but, for the chica heroine, as a deliberate, more open-ended *corrective* to popular images of Latino or Mexican (American) "laziness" and criminality.

The second group includes representations of work in writing by specifically Mexican American authors, including Cano-Murillo and Acosta, who usually present their readers with heroines who are at the beginning of their journeys and thus still in search of that glamorous or at least fulfilling career. As we will see, these characters are often represented as doing kinds of work—sewing, gardening, writing, crafting—that often conjure a feeling of domesticity. Such work is also depicted as the motivating force in leading each heroine on the path to owning businesses or to finding a professional career. That the characters (as well as the authors) are Mexican American is important in noting that the work involved is never presented as manual labor even if, as with gardening, it presumably does involve such. For example, Acosta's second book in her *Happy Hour at Casa Dracula* series begins with Milagro musing on her career as a professional gardener: "My mother Regina would be disgusted that I was laboring 'like an immigrant in the dirt.'" Although Milagro's father had been successful with his own landscaping business, Milagro's mother Regina "equated my proximity [to the soil] with her miserable days as a member of the lower classes" (7). Milagro's work, then, is presented not as manual labor but as reassuringly gendered, creative work that can be leveraged into a profession or a small business. *Waking Up*'s Star, although she has a best friend who is a crafter, wants to consider herself an artist but she must come to the realization that crafting is creative as well. Looking at crafting tools and materials she had originally bought for her friend Ofie (whose own craft creations are hideous), the omniscient narrator tells us that "With all her preaching about art versus craft, Star couldn't be caught dead with these items. . . . [but] if Frida Kahlo lived in this era, perhaps she would use curvy scissors now and then. It wouldn't diminish the seriousness of *her* work" (61). The reference to Kahlo, whose own work appropriated folk and lower-class strategies without apology, and whose paintings now command top dollar, is no accident. At the nadir of Star's young life, with no job, no boyfriend and seemingly no prospects, Kahlo presumably stands for Star as a way to turn ethnic, low-class dross into artistic gold. Star's secret creation of a Mexican-inspired "love shrine" for her ex, Theo, will in due time leverage the "Mexican" part of her heritage into an up-and-coming artistic career. In just two months after she makes her first love shrine, Estrella has crafted twenty-four more boxes, which she is invited to exhibit in a local art gallery called La Pachanga (a Cuban term for a genre of music, but also, in slang, a party) during their Día de los Muertos celebration, where the boxes sell briskly. Explaining them to her father, Star says, "Making these love shrines . . . has taught me that art is about transferring something you are passionate about into something for the senses. . . . As soon as I let go of my stigma about crafts, the creativity rushed in" (202). Presented as each chica's *passion*, work like gardening and crafting thereby avoids or undermines possible connections to the underpaid manual toil imagined as "natural" for lower-class, laboring Mexican Americans. Meanwhile, these activities help our chica heroines to find their "niche" (*Waking Up* 201), in the process showing how even a Mexican American chica can grow up and into a distinctly American entrepreneurial spirit. As we will see next, Marta Acosta has gone further, intertwining aspects of paranormal fiction with questions of how to enact work as a part of "becoming American" in the contemporary US neoliberal landscape.

Paranormal Mexican American Romance

I wanted to do things to Ian Ducharme. . . . I wanted to rip his clothes off and suck the very air out of his lungs like a succubus. I wanted to fall at his feet and submit entirely to his most perverse desires like a minion. I wanted to pin him down and tear into his flesh like a wolf. I wanted to drink his blood and possess him like a vampire.

—Marta Acosta, *Haunted Honeymoon*

It may seem strange to pair a discussion of work, career, and labor conditions with the overwhelming popularity of the paranormal romance—including paranormal chica lit. But as we are beginning to see, because chica lit must address questions of the intersection of race, gender, and ethnicity that no one generic formula can resolve, writers of chica lit tend to pick, choose, and combine generic strategies and assumptions. Acosta, for example, quite cleverly appropriates aspects of a combination of gothic romantic drama, "paranormal" happenings, and the droll repartee and endless mistaken motives of the comedy of manners. She thus manages to insert the requisite broken hearts and often humorous self-deprecation of the main character within an amusing set of situations, lightly sprinkled with a touch of social consciousness, where Milagro's search for her own career, and the meaning of her life, plays out. Thus, understanding the importance of work outside the home to the genre of chica lit is key. As we have seen in the discussion of the career girl novel, the careers, if not actual manual labor, of the chica heroine are just as central to the chica lit story as is the romance.

The spectacular rise of the paranormal romance (in distinction from, though related to, gothic romance) of the last decade or so has yet to be closely examined; thus, I look to the few scholars, such as Young, for ways in which to think about the place of the paranormal romance's assumptions and requirements in twenty-first-century chica lit. Young asserts that "the paranormal romance subgenre that emerges in the 1990s . . . explores the changing constructions of male and female subjectivity under flexible accumulation" (206); yet I argue that such economic and cultural changes began at least as far back as the 1960s, particularly with the insertion of more and more women into the workplace. These changes required a reformation of popular romance's formulaic requirements and, as we will see later, were particularly evident in the rise of the new career girl novel. Here, I show how some of the elements of the paranormal romance can be paired with the concerns of the career girl about work in order to address some of the changes young, especially ethnic, women face in the twenty-first century.

In the *Casa Dracula* series, Milagro falls madly in love with, and is bitten by, a wealthy and handsome man who exhibits all the signs of vampirism. Rescued and nursed back to health by these selfsame vampires, going through physical changes, broken engagements, plot twists and turns, Milagro manages to foil at least two evil groups out to dominate the world by extracting valuable powers from her and her vampire and zombie friends' blood. Understanding persecution as a Mexican American, Milagro can identify with the vampires, and it doesn't hurt that they are rich and good-looking. By the third novel, *Bride of Casa Dracula*, Milagro will emerge as a kind of super–Mexican American *chica* neovampire. She will be stronger than most men, and able to heal at will. Unlike the other vampires, with her Mexican American brown skin she is also able to go out in the sun without big hats and sunscreen. Such abilities, it is hinted, rest on the idea that ethnic peoples are endlessly adaptable: as Milagro notes, "Sebastian had said that my people had the ability to adapt and he was right" (357).

As we near the end of each book in the series, Milagro as well as the reader will be reassured that all her many madcap adventures and forays into different, not very well-paid jobs are not just reiterated parts of a shaggy dog story. Instead, they will lead up to one of the central didactic "teaching" aspects of chica lit; that is, understanding her purpose as a young woman who has successfully integrated "being" Mexican American into what it means to be fully and culturally American, an understanding that has already given her many more options than she had at the beginning of the series. In fact, it is Milagro's various jobs that work as framing schemes for those madcap adventures of hers, which themselves provide the narrative energy to move the story forward to what, clearly, the author of these books knows the chica lit reader herself is trying to figure out. That is, what a chica heroine is to do and to become depends on a socioeconomic system that increasingly demands an "identity" underwritten by a career and franchised and shaped by corporate marketing of multicultural lifestyles.

Acosta's narratives depend on the enormous contemporary appeal of the paranormal romance, and on certain narrative goals that the fictive strategies of paranormal storytelling can help the writer achieve. In chica lit, paranormal plotlines help negotiate the complexities of US cultural imaginaries about the "otherness" or alienness of Latinas as, at the same time, they thread the minefield of contradictory assumptions especially about ethnic femininity and the work role(s) of women in an extended post–Women's Liberation moment. Besides, in a paranormal world such as Acosta's, one gets to meet the most intriguing, darkly handsome, wealthy, and mysterious strangers.

Even before the phenomenal success of Stephenie Meyer's *Twilight* series, paranormal romance's explosion into the publishing world had been giving sagging sales of popular genres a boost (save for romance titles themselves, which actually grew in sales in 2009, immediately after the beginning of the Great Recession). Jessica DiVisconte describes her internship in the midst of the recession at Dorchester, a small press where "any proposed book that could be classified under the paranormal or fantasy romance genres was top priority for both Dorchester's Leisure and Love Spell imprints" (2). In its own blend of genres—a mashup of gothic, fantasy, chick lit, and others—and seemingly endless parade of supernatural creatures, paranormal romance has increased readership among a loyal romance audience but also introduced "non-romance readers to genres within romance" (3).

The reason for the spike in paranormal romance sales since 2009, especially in e-book form, might be explained away as an increased desire for "escapism" and fantasy during hard times. Yet scholars of popular women's genres have shown that the paranormal aspects of romance and chick lit fictions function in specific ways, particularly responding, as we have seen with chica lit, to neoliberal socioeconomic changes. Both Erin Young and Ananya Mukherjea have suggested that part of what the paranormal setting brings to the array of narrative strategies available to women authors is the negotiation of an economy where it is no longer assured that one will stay at one job or career one's whole life—indeed, where it is assumed that most people will have to "remake" themselves several times over in the course of their working lives. Neither Acosta's chica heroine nor the chicas of Castillo's *Switchcraft* become supernatural beings themselves (Milagro gains certain powers but, as she herself protests, is certainly not a paranormal chica). Yet although Young discusses novels where young women actually become, for example, werewolf-women who (unlike Milagro, or Aggie and Nely of *Switchcraft*) reject both marriage and reproduction, her observations are again valuable for thinking about how work and gender roles ultimately shape an ethnic femininity in the *Casa Dracula* series. Although Milagro's superhuman strength and ability to heal instantly does seem to erode the divisions of labor of "contemporary gendered realms," access to her vampire lovers' seemingly unlimited resources insures the heroine against the specter of failure because of her downgraded financial circumstances, and ensures her "freedom" to be romantically coupled with them.

Additionally, paranormal romance advances the assumption that the extended lives of such creatures as werewolves and vampires will inevitably lead to material wealth and ease. As Young notes in her examination of werewolf romances, "The werewolf Pack, which has existed for centuries, has accumulated a great deal of wealth. As a high-ranking member of this Pack, Elena has access to its financial resources: 'Jeremy's bank account was also in my name and Clay's, allowing any of us to withdraw money for household needs.' Household needs, for these werewolves, include sports cars and designer clothing" (210). Like Young's werewolves, both Milagro and her "neovampires" see themselves as having a treatable yet incurable disease. Yet for Milagro, being bitten (twice) and surviving (by reason, it is hinted, of her Mexican American heritage) means she now has the gift of abnormal strength and instant healing powers, supercharging an already resistant immune system. In this sense, by the end of the fourth book Milagro, if not immortal, at least will have an extended life, like the werewolves Young describes. Indeed, like these werewolves, her strength and "recuperative abilities render death . . . a minor concern" (202). Like the werewolves, Milagro has always been immune to disease (she's never been ill until her "fever" after first being bitten). Yet the sexual freedom this affords Milagro, and which she deploys throughout the series, is finally put in the service of her "true love" for Ducharme, because she can now match his strength and instantly heal from the cuts he inflicts on her in their passion. In this sense, Milagro's independence and her adaptability in the face of new economic structures are made to fit with publishing requirements that women's special powers—whatever they might be—be used in the service of heterosexual romance and even reproduction.

This same observation applies to Milagro's college education. Education at a Fancy University is still of great importance to the characters of many other chica lit novels. Milagro constantly looks for a career suitable for a chica with a Fancy University degree, but unlike other chica lit novels that tend to fetishize Ivy League degrees, her education is increasingly portrayed in this paranormal chica story not just as valueless but as inappropriate for a moment when the seeming verities of Fordist production have given way to a much more unstable era of flexible accumulation. But even though Acosta's Milagro is clearly cast within the vagaries of flexible accumulation, as a Mexican American character the exigencies of the romance narrative will help prove her femininity at the same time that her paranormal adventures provide her with various kinds of work.

As Acosta herself has noted, the vampires and zombies, and the people out to destroy them, are ways of making the reader aware of "otherness" and prejudice. Indeed, Acosta sets up a madcap series of plots that allows her Mexican American heroine to voice some resistance to anti-Mexican-American racism, if not to anti-*Mexican* sentiment, in the United States. To do this, she makes a parallel between anti-Mexican racism and Milagro's connection with another "persecuted" group—the vampires, who in *Casa Dracula* are being pursued by her ex-boyfriend and Sebastian and his evil organization, Corporate Americans for the Conservation of America (CACA for short, or "shit" in Spanish). CACA wants to capture vampires in order to find and engineer the genetic anomaly that makes them what they are (348). The lore about vampires is also presented as prejudicial. Gabriel, a gay vampire, chastises Milagro for being insensitive about vampires (and homosexuality), saying, "I told you, we don't 'suck blood.' I would think that a woman of color would understand prejudice" (69). After she is first "infected" with vampire blood, Gabriel and Milagro argue about who is more persecuted, Gabriel saying,

> "You have no idea what it's like to fall for someone who will never accept you because you were born different!"
> "Ha," I said, "and ha again. . . . I think I know what it's like to be outside the norm. And besides, being a vampire is completely different from being an ethnic minority."
> "We are *not* vampires," he snapped back. "At least your people can intermarry and be open about who they are and share their culture." (70)

Acosta's Milagro takes visible pride in being Mexican, and throughout the four novels of the series Milagro is shown, albeit either clumsily or humorously, to be sensitive to derogatory references about her "Mexicanness." For example, in *Casa Dracula* she is installed in the maid's room at her vampire lover Oswald's ranch—a fact which will, in *Bride of Casa Dracula*, cause a werewolf plastic surgeon named Dr. Vidalia ("like the onion") to actually mistake her for the maid rather than for

Oswald's fiancée. Again, when Milagro is captured by Sebastian for the purposes of experimentation, he says, "Milagro, I reject you and all creatures of darkness," she snaps back, "Is that a swipe at me for being Latina?!" Sebastian's answer makes the parallel between "persecuted" groups clear: "'Spare me your politically correct outrage,' he sneered. 'I was referring to your vampire-tainted flesh'" (61).

Here vampires, like Mexican Americans, are explicitly characterized as a persecuted group tied closely to each other by (pseudo-racial) bloodlines. In fact, the vampires cannot usually, save for Oswald and Milagro's case, marry "outside" the vampire clan, either since most humans die from being "infected" or because vampire-human children have a 25 percent mortality rate. Vampires also have low fertility rates, and so must be matched according to the best statistics for fertility—a strangely eugenicist vision for Acosta's critique of anti-miscegenation sentiments (141). The reader discovers however that not all the vampires are equally beneficial creatures. The "good" ones, such as Milagro's intended vampire family, think of themselves as "neo-vampires," and consider their vampiric attributes as characteristics of an inherited disease; they use sunscreen to go out in the sun and they drink only the blood of well-cared-for animals, and try to avoid "infecting" humans. Others, however, among them the fascinating Ian Ducharme, embrace the standard vampire lore, particularly in their willingness to drink human blood from "thralls." The vampire Council especially is pictured as conservative and at least creepy, if not possibly evil. Because the Council decides, among other things, on the suitability of vampire marriages, in *Bride* Milagro, who is engaged to Oswald, must meet with the Council, as they are doubtful of "mixed marriages" and particularly, it is implied, of Milagro's class and racial suitability for her wealthy plastic surgeon fiancé (all the vampires appear to be white).

Here, Acosta's critique of racial fears of miscegenation underscores her rejection of the notion that Mexican Americans are racially inferior, either because they themselves are "mixed" or because they should not mix with whites. But the worst is yet to come when the Council demands that Milagro sign a "loyalty oath" in which she pledges allegiance to the vampire "nation," renouncing in the process her American citizenship:

> I skimmed the page and one phrase jumped out: "do hereby re-
> nounce all allegiance to any other nation." I was angry. . . . "I'm not
> giving up my citizenship."
> "Think about it. After all, this country has not exactly welcomed
> *your* people. They'll always see you as a second-class citizen because
> of the color of your skin and your name." . . .
> "That may be true, but what matters is my love for this country and
> its ideals." (301)

Yet despite the apparent importance of such a scene, her dangerous
vampire swain Ian Ducharme appears and distracts her completely
with his (du)charm, and the problem of what to do with her Americanness is virtually forgotten; we are assured that she will, despite
US suspicions of her, remain a faithful citizen. The books' references
to Milagro's social consciousness around race and ethnicity (though
rarely around gender; feminism, as with many of these novels, is
apparently a done deal) raise an oddly discordant note. Milagro is
a power for good—she saves people who are murdered by turning
them into peaceful, happy zombies with her shaman's gift of an herb-
enhanced veil, for example, and all her paid work benefits others. Thus
a certain amount of ideological tension is produced by the gap between the series' insistence that Milagro is loyally American despite
US anti-Mexican racism, her awareness of said racism, her adaptability to an economy of flexible accumulation, and her insistence that she
is a wacky girl who "just wants to have fun" (*Bride* 310). Similarly, her
insistence that she is not interested in money exists in tension with
the novels' ongoing gothic romance plot, which insists that she par-
take of the wealth made freely available to her by the two astoundingly
wealthy, handsome, and sexy vampires romantically interested in her.

By Acosta's third *Casa Dracula* novel, *Midnight Brunch*, we see
how Milagro's endless zany adventures with persecuted "neovampires," secret organizations out for world domination, shapeshifters,
werewolves, friendly zombies, and Don Juan–like shamans are structured around and through her entrance into flexible accumulation via
the many and varied jobs, mostly writing and gardening, she can scrape
together or be offered. Through a truly improbable series of circumstances (not that the vampire plotline is not improbable in itself, but in
a different way), Milagro by this time has had enough labor experience

to be able to sum up her current value as a working girl: "I now knew that I was a good teacher. I applied to a graduate program so I could start working on my credentials through extension courses" (322); she can also ghostwrite books and rewrite screenplays, although other less scrupulous characters get most of the credit and the money from these. Finally, there's her love of gardening. A fabulously wealthy and fabulous woman, Gigi, who has befriended her over the course of the book, pays her with a "generous check" for a landscape design, which her fabulous and fabulously wealthy vampire fiancé urges her to accept, since "It's like prostitution—if you don't get paid you're just an enthusiastic amateur" (324).

At this point in the series Milagro feels a sense of pride in her own journey toward a productive profession (even if it has been strangely likened to prostitution by her wealthy fiancé). As she notes, "A job here and a job there, and I've been cobbling together a living even if I still can't devote myself to one career." Yet this working-chica self-sufficiency, even connected as it is to a (muffled) ethnic consciousness, does not ultimately stand in the way of her enjoyment of the money with which others are willing to shower her: "I haven't used the credit card Oswald gave me," Milagro muses in *Midnight*, "but I'm more open-minded about sharing the wealth" (324).

Aside from the many adventures she experiences through her jobs, her own paranormal powers boosted by her vampire lovers allow her not only certain freedoms but a way to both acknowledge her "race" and make it, finally, a nonissue. Through the narrative's promise that Milagro will "end up" with one or the other of her equally fantastic vampire lovers, Milagro is relatively free to, for example, have great sex with a younger, surfer neovampire, negotiating her own relationship to "gendered prescriptions [and] proscriptions." She learns along the way that she cannot be the "serious" young lady she should have learned to be; instead, she must be true to the fun—and sex-loving—chica she is. Here, "seriousness" is subliminally connected to whiteness, while Milagro's totally nonserious, madcap nature is overtly connected to her Mexican Americanness. Yet she must still struggle with the lived contradictions of being a young, well-educated Mexican American woman in a downward economy. Here, the "vampire boyfriend" is "a vehicle that allows the author and the reader to indulge a craving for an old-fashioned, generally wealthy, and socially dominant gentleman and a fantasy of stable and secure gendered expectations without fundamentally compromising or relinquishing hard-won and necessary, but also sometimes challenging, feminist rights and responsibilities" (Mukherjea 1). After many false starts and mistaken motivations, Milagro finally comes to understand that the "real" vampire Ian Ducharme, who fits the "old-fashioned, generally wealthy, and socially dominant gentleman" description to a T, is her forever soulmate. By the end of the fourth book, they are married and, deliriously happy, literally setting off into the sunset together. As Mukherjea puts it, "the desire for a vampire boyfriend has to do with the contradictory and conflicted relationship that many women have to feminism and femininity and a perceived conflict between feeling protected and having the approval of visible femininity, on the one hand, and being self-determining and active, on the other" (3). Such a conflicted relationship, for Milagro, includes her racial and ethnic status in the United States.

Having the titled and wealthy Ian Ducharme as her willing lover, Milagro has the freedom to choose (or choose not) to exercise her autonomy in pursuing her not particularly lucrative careers as writer and landscape gardener, while being protected and cossetted in his wealth and power. According to Mukherjea, in the vampire romance—more traditionally "romantic," interestingly, than the werewolf narratives that Young examines—the use of the paranormal as a writerly strategy allows for a useful blurring of the boundaries found in more traditional women's popular narratives: "A paranormal figure is ideal for playing the multi-faceted, constantly evolving, but deeply reliable male lead for today's postfeminist heroine as she navigates the shifting array of gendered prescriptions, proscriptions, and desires before her" (4).

Yet even as Acosta uses the paranormal to destabilize many of the traditional romance's more rigid assumptions about gender, labor, and race, an emphasis on heterosexual romance and material success were requirements for publishing, as she has noted. Here again, Milagro's search for the proper career path for a modern but ethnically aware young woman is driven at least in part by her encounters with different men. Her first vampire lover Oswald's bite sends her on her journey of discovery and independence, Ian DuCharme opens her sexually to a wild side she didn't know she had, evil Sebastian provides the focal point for her quest against persecution and corporate greed. But despite a few protestations of class unease, these men's wealth—for example, she is allowed to spend much of her time at the luxe "ranch" where Oswald lives—allows Milagro the space to insert herself into a neoliberal regime of flexible accumulation, at the same time that her vampire lovers' wealth and luxury provide wildly seductive scenes of love and desire. The uncomfortable fit between these two plot patterns comes to a head when, introduced to the extravagantly lavish house her newly wedded husband DuCharme has bought for them, Milagro reminds him she didn't marry him for his money. DuCharme, answering that he knows "exactly" what she wants—"It's in my pants"—carries her to "a sumptuous ivory and moss green bedroom and la[id her] on the bed. Candles in silver candlesticks flickered their warm light, a bottle of champagne rested in a wine cooler, and there were vases of antique roses in creamy colors" (305). Admittedly, it would be hard to resist access to such seductive trappings, underscored by the fact that DuCharme also owns a Caribbean island in "azure waters"— although he holds the title only to "protect the true owners, a tribe with a name that could only be sounded with whistles" (305). No matter Acosta's original and more radical intentions, finally, other people's money and privileges, it turns out, can be enjoyed without too many problems from one's social conscience, especially when they come with a penchant for doing good. On the penultimate page, Milagro sums up for us what she has gained: "Before meeting the vampires . . . I dreamed of being in love with a fabulous but worthy man and being loved in return. . . . I dreamed of making a difference. And all those things had come true for me. . . . I'd made a difference. I'd united couples, created gardens, and thwarted the dangerous ambitions of madmen, death merchants, and extremists, while always finding time for friends and fun" (309–10). Problems and contradictions inherent in the publishing world's requirements end in prescriptive representations of Americanized, often ethnically unmarked Latinas. Such contradictions necessitate chica lit's borrowings of genre elements from several categories of women's popular fiction. Although this mashup of generic conventions still functions to represent Latinas within the confines of mass-market narrative and production requirements, a few writers such as Acosta manage to insert some recognizable moments of resistance to assimilative efforts.

As I have been arguing, however, chica lit presents itself not just as a fun read but also as a site of learning. In the next chapter, I discuss chica lit's investment in the concept of the "culture of poverty," and its borrowing of questions of class, style, and taste from chick lit. Even more importantly, these aspects of chica lit provide the material for object lessons in the significance of class and material achievements for a commodifiable ethnicity and a cultural Americanization.

Chapter 2

Class and Taste: Is It the Poverty?

The ascendency of neoliberalism, in turn, has been characterized
by a diminished space for discussing issues of social welfare and
justice. Poverty has become the ultimate unredeemable liability for
which the only response is to emphasize the political rentability
and marketability of particular groupings.

—ARLENE DÁVILA, *LATINO SPIN*

The plots of chica lit fiction often assume, as both background and
foil to its chica heroines' material and romantic successes, that among
poor and even working-class Latinos/as or Mexican Americans there
exists a "culture of poverty." This notion was made famous by the anthropologist Oscar Lewis, first in a sociological study of Mexicans in
1961 called *Five Families: Mexican Case Studies in the Culture of Poverty* and continued in other works, including his best-known study,
*La Vida: A Puerto Rican Family in the Culture of Poverty—San Juan
and New York*, of 1966. Lewis was in fact on the front lines of the war
against poverty in the 1950s and '60s, and believed wholeheartedly
that poverty was the result of systemic problems rather than individual faults. Lewis also believed, nevertheless, that generational poverty
over time could generate its own "subculture." As Lewis wrote in the
October 1966 issue of *Scientific American*, "In my writings [the term
'culture of poverty' means] . . . a subculture of Western society with
its own structure and rationale, a way of life handed on from generation to generation along family lines. . . . [I]t provides human beings

with a design for living, with a ready-made set of solutions for human problems, and so serves a significant adaptive function" (19). By the early 1970s, the idea of a "culture of poverty" had begun to lose favor with policymakers and academics alike. Nevertheless, despite Lewis's assertions that it had been much misused, this idea, especially minus Lewis's belief that poverty was a social rather than an individual problem, has persisted in the popular imagination as an explanation for why poor people stay poor, and it has had a lively presence in assertions of the "inevitability" of poverty itself, especially for African Americans. However, Lewis's work mostly with Mexicans and Puerto Ricans makes the (mis)use of this term a particularly attractive strategy for chica lit, given chica lit's insistence on, again, the inevitability of material success for those chica heroines who—despite setbacks and even personal failings and mistakes—learn how to wrest themselves from Latino "stereotypes" and make themselves into Americans.

Here, chica lit activates two seemingly opposing, yet actually connected, US imaginaries around the presumed class status of Latinas/os. The first is an image of a Latina/o population as *born* to be laboring, working poor, or worse, birthed in barrios where a perverse attitude of resistance to success comes with the package. This is the imaginary against which these novels must construct their counter-representation of Latina success. Chica lit heroines are either born into middle- and upper-middle-class families and, despite their problems, learn how to leverage their Latina "heritage" in order to preserve their generational wealth, or are strivers from poor or otherwise disadvantaged backgrounds who learn, from the lessons of disillusion and disappointment, how to bootstrap themselves into lasting material success.

First in this chapter, we see how the notion of an ethnic culture of poverty works as a cautionary and so didactic tale for the chica heroine. From questions of ethnic poverty, we will then turn to the place of ethnic, particularly Mexican, kitsch in the American imaginary. The notion of *kitsch*, the German word for items that are popular, cheap, and marketable, has interested sociologists as a concept that works as a convenient shorthand for class-based hierarchies of taste and style. As the French sociologist Pierre Bourdieu has shown, in fact, taste is not merely a matter of knowing what "looks good"; it is the material sign of material inequities, and as such, ensures that these inequities stay in place. One only has to think of terms like "nouveau riche" or "ghetto fabulous" to understand that wealth does not necessarily open the doors to social equality. The concept of kitsch has its roots in a classed rejection of mass production. For gatekeepers of class hierarchies, the concept of art as a unique, precious, and therefore expensive thing is threatened if not extinguished by the advent of the taste for mass market, cheaply produced goods. A late twentieth-century enthusiasm for the "retro," rediscovered in working-class tastes and mass-produced goods particularly from the postwar and midcentury years, is rooted in the gravitation toward sentimentality and in the nostalgia, for example, for the outdated yet imagined stability of these time periods. Here, then, the deliberate revaluation of the outdated and the lowbrow is reborn as a kitsch sensibility—a sense of style which may be expressed with a distancing irony as camp, or which may be expressed as a close embrace of the cheap and the sentimental.

For Mexican American heroines, evocations of Mexico must be handled with care, lest they become associated with imaginaries about a Mexican "culture" of poverty, violence, and drugs. Thus, I argue that the "Mexicanness" of Mexican American characters must be reassociated with another familiar US cultural imaginary: the turn toward Mexican kitsch. This is centered on images of a Mexico where cheap, colorful, and bizarrely appealing goods—elaborate, highly colored decorative motifs on skulls, colorful cut tinware, *milagritos* of hands, arms, and legs, bright clothing and houses, and comic book *telenovelas* jostle with the ubiquitous presence of Frida Kahlo self-portraits miniaturized and stuck onto any available surface. Such objects, I argue, are recycled to evoke associations with bygone days when Mexico was an inexpensive tourist "land that time forgot."

As I have been emphasizing, chica lit must raise the specter of ethnic poverty or ethnic resistance—the two are sometimes conflated—in order to instruct both heroine and reader how to avoid or transcend such states. At the same time, the class concerns of chick lit and romance are also triggered in chica lit. As primary consumers, women's class status is also reified by their sense of décor (taste) and wardrobe (style), and again, these novels must address the vexed question of what an American ethnicity might look like. As scholars of contemporary popular women's writing agree, chica lit and chick lit fiction privileges "style" and taste as central concerns for their characters to such a degree that characters' senses of taste—and with it, class—come to represent their very subjectivity, not to mention ideological orientations. Harzewski's reminder that "the reifying values of the marketplace and the sovereignty of style permeate how the chick lit protagonist perceives herself, her stratagems, and the judgment of her peers" is as salient for chica as it is for chick lit (*Chick Lit and Postfeminism* 302).[1]

Mexican American authors, however, must deal with the specter of Mexican poverty and illegality infecting, so to speak, their own representations of Mexican American chica heroines. Thus, these texts show how to Latinize the presumably fun and nonthreatening kitschiness of "Mexican" culture into an easily commodified personal style whose colorful playfulness acts to moderate the apparent threats posed by a real and contemporary Mexico.

Uplifting Chicas

In chica lit, images of poor Latinas/os, grounded as they are in the rhetoric of a "culture of poverty," fixes on ethnic poverty as the cause for the "stereotyping" of Latinos/as in general. In some instances, the remedy for this problem is the emulation of the tenets of African American racial uplift. In chica lit, then, (often ungrateful) Latinos and Chicanas are mentored, occasionally to their own middle-class success—eliding altogether the fact of the backward pull that generational poverty can have. Often, however, the individual chica heroine's attempt at uplifting "one of her own" ends in abject failure. Further, in chica lit fiction such as that of Lara Rios and Alisa Valdes, the requirement that one participate in mentoring the poor clashes strangely with the narratives' insistence on the importance to Latinas in general of access to a level of luxury which assumes a more than middle-class budget.

As I have been emphasizing, it is easier for these novels to show how *not* to do ethnicity; this is achieved through a negative investment on the part of authors and chica lit characters alike in ethnic resistance to a dominant Anglo world. Most of all, these novels are notable in their almost complete rejection of the ethnic resistance to structures of oppression that has been a hallmark of a "conscious" ethnicity since the beginning of the 1970s. In fact, how and whether you can be both ethnic and American has been central to Chicana/o *mov-imiento* discourses from the 1960s through the 1980s (and has been carried on in ideological public battles over the status of Latinas/os in the United States since the '90s). For example, one of several threads in Chicano cultural nationalist rhetoric involved an emphasis on, and reclamation of, the Chicano's "Aztec" roots, at once a radical repudiation of white supremacy and a claiming of a homeland, Aztlán, within the larger nation-state. Indeed, such a radicalized reclamation of identity is taken up in chica lit, but only within the context of an invidious comparison. For example, when *Becoming Latina*'s Marcela asks her "Chicana activist" Aunt Lydia to tell her "what the Chicano movement is all about" her aunt replies, "[Chicanos] continue to . . . make sure no one forgets that this [California] is our homeland." At this juncture, we are cut off from Aunt Lydia's presumably old school, sadly mistaken views of Chicano autonomy when Marcela immediately thinks, "She wasn't going to get agreement from me on this point. That California was once part of Mexico in the early 1800s had little to do with our life today. To me this was *my* homeland. . . . It's part of America—my country" (128). Thankfully, we never hear from Aunt Lydia again.

Again, when *Dirty Girls*'s Mexican American character Amber assumes the Nahuatl name Cuicatl and begins to campaign for Native American awareness through her life and music, Lauren mocks her efforts: "I call Amber at home. She answers her phone in a language I've never heard before, I'm assuming it's Nahuatl. . . . 'Hey, Amber, it's me, Lauren.' 'Please call me Cuicatl,' she says. 'That's my new name. I'm not a part-time Indian, so don't treat me like one.'" At this point, Lauren thinks, "'Humorless as always,' [and says to Cuicatl,] 'I would if I could pronounce it, okay, girl?' . . . She doesn't laugh. Ever since she got caught up in all this Mexica movement stuff she hasn't seemed to have much of a sense of humor" (288). As Debra Castillo notes in her brilliant essay "Impossible Indian," the novel presents Cuicatl/Amber's devotion to her Native American roots as "comically exaggerated" (52), ensuring that the reader knows not to take Amber seriously. As Castillo notes, Cuicatl/Amber is taken up with the question of (historical) cultural authenticity: "For Amber, the goal of dominant culture to 'disappear us' and the problem of the fake Indian are closely allied. 'Don't trust indios falsos,' she warns her friends, and she describes the indio falso as someone 'in denial of your beautiful brown roots': that is, a real Indian with assimilationist values" (54). To make matters worse, Amber/Cuicatl makes no money with her music. Thus, the novel's own investment in middle-class ethnic success sets up Amber's involvement in the Mexica movement as the single most wrong-headed way to do an ethnic "Latina" identity. Instead, by the end of the novel, when Cuicatl has achieved a successful recording career with a multimillion-dollar recording contract, the narrative is careful to make its readers understand that her success—and getting her "message" out to the most people—must involve the sacrifice of a resistant stance. She finally accepts the record company's insistence that she sing in English rather than Spanish or Nahuatl; she no longer has a problem with Shakira or similar singers bleaching their hair blonde (something against which she had previously railed), and she has finally embraced the necessary trappings of a successful "Latina." Her picture is now on the cover of *Ella*. Lauren sums it up: "Cuicatl— I've finally learned to say her name, okay, because it's impossible not to with every teenager on the street shouting it—comes . . . in a white stretch limo . . . she says . . . it's about time a Mexica got to ride in style" (37).

Yet in the midst of all this ethnic success, Debra Castillo notes, "The problem [Cuicatl/Amber] does not address . . . is to what degree maintaining an imperfectly consolidated performative self substitutes for . . . historical losses and comprises a real autonomy" (54). Because novels such as these are *themselves* concerned with the performance of a suitable ethnic identity, their jibes at the identities that come out of a more radical *movimiento* politics are meant to point to the ridiculously performative nature of a *resistant* ethnic self, constructed through appeals to "authenticity." Part of this problem is a late twentieth-century, ideologically conservative turn to a neoliberal sense of self, one that works to (re)privatize the sense of an ethnically gendered self within a world where, if you follow the rules, there will be seemingly endless life and consumer choices. In this world, the sometimes separatist and always oppositional ethnic identities created in the 1960s and '70s seem not only out of place but almost impossible, if not downright embarrassing, to perform. Such a comparison reinforces not just the inevitability—the rightness, one might say—of a market-driven sense of ethnicity, but also engages the reader in agreement about how much more pleasurable it is to do a gendered ethnicity that, instead of insisting on loss, will bring you success, shopping, and romance.

Thus, in many of these novels, the creation of a twenty-first-century women's *latinidad* engages in a negative identification with what are variously seen as stereotypical, poverty-ridden, "ghetto," or, most especially, unassimilable ethnic behaviors. For example, the characters—as well as their authors—often militate against the idea that speaking Spanish is necessary; indeed, it might be the ticket to middle-class success, as Mary Castillo's character Isela Vargas discovers in the short story "My Favorite Mistake." As Isela tells it, not without a bit of tongue-in-cheek humor, "In college, I was laughed away from the MEChA table at Freshman Orientation for not speaking Spanish. I showed them and joined the Latino Business Student Association" (16).[2] Asserting the outmoded nature of such cultural markers as speaking Spanish, chica lit often invites comparisons between behaviors that might keep a Latina stuck in a "culture of poverty," and those leading to material and romantic success as a cultural American.

Several scholars have already noted this strategy at work in Valdes's writing, citing Lauren's assertions in *Dirty Girls* about the *sucias'* professional status, rather than the "stereotypical" immigrants her boss presumably imagines all Latinas are: "brown of face and hair, uniformly uneducated, swarming across the border . . . with all their belongings in plastic grocery bags" (7). Critics such as Hurt and Morrison have also noted Valdes's thinly veiled references to the Chicana writer Denise Chávez, author of *Loving Pedro Infante, The Last of the Menu Girls*, and *Face of an Angel*, whose writings about working-class women seem especially to have raised Lauren's ire and her corrective descriptions of her *sucias'* achievements. Lauren's anger seems outsized enough, unfortunately, for the reader to feel that the stereotypical thinking she so scornfully ascribes to her editor is in fact Lauren's own, although Valdes surely did not intend for this effect.

Nor does Valdes put aside such comments in her second book, *Playing with Boys*. Here, the Tejana protagonist Alexis is a Southern Methodist University graduate and self-described "sorority sister" publicist for a well-known band called Los Chimpances del Norte. When she sets them up to play for a benefit (and here again, the insider will understand Valdes to be referencing the real-life and extraordinarily successful Mexican *conjunto* Los Tigres del Norte, who as young boys crossed over into the States from Mexico, and who ended up living—illegally—in California), she is horrified to see that they have refused to wear the Armani suits she picked out for them. Instead, they are wearing their own down-market clothes, complete with enormous, tacky, Mexican-flag belt buckles. When she protests to Filoberto, the bandleader, this dialogue ensues: "Filoberto stared hard into my eyes. 'Look,' he said, in the perfect English he often pretended he didn't speak. . . . '*Mexicans* gave us the money. . . . we owe our careers to *Mexicans*. We are *Mexicans*. And we're not going to dress like gringos just to make your little ooh-ooh friends here comfortable'" (7). Although this sounds as though Filoberto is making a move toward a resistant cultural stance, the authorial point of such resistance fails. As with all chica lit, this narrative failure arises because it is conservative Alexis, one of the book's main characters, with whom the book has established the reader's sympathy. Thus, Filoberto's position is immediately undercut for the reader by Alexis's own inner thoughts as she walks away: "Blah, blah, blah. Filoberto still thought we were fighting the Alamo" (7). One of the problems with Valdes's writing— snarky, funny, and even laugh-out-loud as it often is—is that it's difficult to tell when, or if, as an author she is lampooning the heroine for her uptight, conservative ways—for example, Alexis or Lauren—or making fun particularly of Mexican and Mexican American characters—such as Filoberto and his band.

As I have noted, the broader generic strategies of popular women's fiction almost universally encourage the reader to identify with the heroine. Thus, even when (as with Lauren in *Dirty Girls Social Club*) she is clearly jealous, wrong, or even self-destructive, our sympathies must be with her, and we know that the chica heroine will learn her lessons and come out on top at the end. These instilled reading practices almost guarantee that in the above scene from *Playing with Boys* the reader will assume that Filoberto is not to be taken seriously. The fact that he can speak perfect English but often pretends not to seems to indicate a faux authenticity, he and his band dress in a ridiculous manner, and, after all, they call themselves the "Chimpanzees of the North." The reader thus understands that her interpretation of the preceding scene must lie with Alexis, whose only moment of pride in being Mexican was "when Vincente Fernández sang 'Cielito Lindo' for the Republican Convention in 2000" (1).

As Amanda María Morrison has shown in her "Chicanas and 'Chick Lit': Contested Latinidad in the Novels of Alisa Valdes-Rodriguez," these novels' invidious comparisons between the straw man of Mexican American "culture" and the books' imaginings of the lives of urban, educated, professional chicas are in fact invidious for a reason: "By emphasizing the upper-class urbanity, youthful sex-appeal and Anglo-normative 'all-American-ness' of her characters, Valdes-Rodriguez and her commercial boosters position her for optimal cross-over potential. Her sanitized version of Latinidad is free of the putatively quaint, old-fashioned, unsophisticated, unassimilated, working-class connotations so often identified with Greater Mexico today" (327). Consumption, class, and poverty work in some of the same ways through Argentinian American Lara Rios's Mexican American heroine of *How to Become Latina in Ten Easy Steps*, Marcela. Unlike Alexis, however, in this case the chica in question is actually trying, albeit haplessly, to construct a sense of ethnicity—but this attempt is mostly through consumption. Indeed, Philips points out that in so-called "shopping" novels, consumption is often not merely confined to objects, but extends to men: "Shopping for men . . . is both about employing consumer skills in order to identify (or even create) an appropriate partner. . . . [and] also the opportunity to select from a range of different men" (240). As we saw in the introduction, Marcela is presented as casting about in various amusing or clueless directions for ways to become Latina and accomplish the tasks she sets herself—particularly number one, "Date Mexican men" (22). Marcela drives a BMW, she is the top animator at her company, and as one of the things on her ethnic to-do list, she has enough money to hire a chef to personally teach her how to cook Mexican food. Most importantly, she is on the lookout for the correct Latino boyfriend to top off her search for a reconnection to her "roots." Yet the traces of the traditional romance formula found in chica lit ensure that the reader will "know," or at least be able to guess with some certainty, certain outcomes long before the heroine herself experiences them. As the search for a suitable ethnic identity will lead chica lit characters to "shop around" for suitably ethnic men, the reader will intuit ahead of the character which man will in fact be the right one. Sometimes, as in *Becoming*, it is the man who has initially been discarded because he is too middle-class and not ethnic enough. At other times, in a reversal that often signals an attempt at racial uplift, he is not suitable because he is *too* ethnic: he is a ghetto drug dealer like *Dirty Girls*'s Amaury. In fact, poor, too-ethnic men play an important role in the narrative mapping of women's ethnic success as Americans.

Transformed into the appropriate man or not, as the figure of ghetto or barrio poverty, these characters demonstrate Latino association with the culture of poverty. Yet, as Lauren decides to do with Amaury, saving one of these creatures can be a way for the chica lit heroine to show how, as a middle-class American, she can engage in the uplift of those who are too poor and too ethnic to become not just legal but cultural Americans on their own. In fact, getting to know, and in the process reshaping, the barrio character need not happen only with men in these novels. As part of her search for an ethnic identity, Marcela decides to mentor an "at-risk" Mexican American girl, Lupe Perez, although her efforts are almost foiled by the girl's Mexican mother, who accuses Marcela of shaming her in front of her daughter. Here, Marcela vocalizes the very essence of the idea of a culture of poverty: "So, what, she wants to keep her daughter poor and uneducated so that she will not look down on her mother? I don't get it" (224). After a rocky start, however, Lupe's mother (and homicidal brother) are left behind, never to be heard from again; Marcela succeeds in lifting the young barrio girl from poverty. Indeed, Rios's next novel, *Becoming Americana* (2006), chronicles now-uplifted Lupe's own coming of age into Americanization—despite the fact that Lupe is, of course, already American, having been born in the United States. Similarly, in *Dirty Girls*, Amber/Cuicatl gets Amaury a straight job promoting her new album, which then leads to a job offer from the "head of Latin marketing for Wagner" (read Warner) records (305).

Of Valdes's characters, Afro–Puerto Rican, barrio-born Usnavys exhibits the most awareness of structural racism—she "hires only Latinas for the assistant jobs under her, including ones less qualified than other applicants. . . . She laughs and says the white boys do it all the time and she's just making up for past injustices" (15). Usnavys attended Harvard for an MBA on a scholarship, but has "issues" about money; her style is "ghetto fabulous" and she refuses to take the tags off new clothing so she can return the items later (12). This behavior in fact proves to be a harbinger of downward mobility for Usnavys, who like other chica lit characters from the barrio cannot always escape their "culture." By the third novel, she is in foreclosure and facing bankruptcy. This is a far cry from the Manolo Blahniks and fur coats of the Usnavys we first see in *Dirty Girls Social Club*, yet the loss of her job cannot quite explain the slip in Usnavys' diction: "We don't even bother to open them notices from the bank no more. We know what they say. They say, get out. They say, America changed when none all y'all was looking" (*Lauren's Saints* np). As we will see with Amaury's character, you can take the girl out of the ghetto, but you can't take the ghetto out of the girl: by the end of this book Usnavys is back on her feet again but in a distinctly more "real" black and ethnic business: she will be the publicist for a neighborhood beauty shop owner, demonstrating the adaptability and entrepreneurship long associated with underclass ethnic striving. But, as befits the chica lit map for success, she understands it's about reshaping oneself. As she informs the owner, Taina, "It's all about branding, girl. You gotta get you a good name, a niche market, a pretty and effective product, and you get out there and you make it happen" (np).

Scholars of chick and chica lit have noted the long lists of designer labels in "shopping novels." These are narratives in which, as Philips notes, "Female friendship is . . . expressed in terms of shared tastes and consumption patterns" (247). As we have seen before, according to Philips, the fashioning of shopping into a means of self-identification and even subjectivity extends to "shopping" for the right man. Yet almost until the very end of such novels, these women still cannot seem to find, or sometimes to recognize, the "right man"; this allows them to try out at least two or three men in the course of the book, although they are ultimately returned (without refunds, alas) when the real one comes along. Thus, like the conflicting demands of financial independence and domestic bliss confronted by the women in Philips's analysis of "single woman" narratives, the reader always understands that "Consumption is offered . . . as a means of reconciling these conflicting demands and of achieving a resolution." Again, the resolution is about possibility and options; if, like Usnavys, the chica heroine is not exactly presented "with an apparent infinite variety of lifestyle . . . [and] consumer choices" (Philips 249), she is presented as now having the possibility of an open-ended future, unlike the closed future of the ethnic culture of poverty.

The preoccupation with class and poverty in chica lit is part and parcel of its necessary appeal to the experiences of the reader. Yet because the available pool of Latinos in reality includes many poor men, shopping for the right man in chica lit can sometimes pose a downright danger when the chica heroine is attracted especially to barrio or ghetto boys. The chica lit discourse of poverty tends to mark poor Latinos as (sexually) dangerous, thus demonstrating through Latinas' "lessons" with these men how deeply inculcated is the "culture of poverty" as well as mapping the ways *not* to go romantically. This fits, for example, the experiences of Marcela in *Becoming Latina*, whose number one item on her list to become Latina is "date Mexican men." Thus, when Marcela decides she must "shop around" for the man who will make her more Latina, she is initially attracted to George "from accounting" who is "Mexican, I think. . . . He's cute, single, and dresses neat" (30). However, as readers we know it's too soon for her and George to get together: she feels that that George won't do since, ironically enough, he is "way too Americanized. He couldn't wow my family with revolutionary talk of Aztec kings" (120). Instead, and against the warnings of her best friend, she decides to make a date with Armando, a "dangerous," poor Chicano gangbanger, a *vato loco*, in an effort to understand what "real Chicanos" are, whom she imagines are "dark, muscular, hot guys who could easily fulfill a girl's wildest fantasies" (65). She thinks, "What drives them? Is it the poverty? Is it a sense of not belonging to society? . . . maybe if I can date and understand a real Chicano, I can better understand. . . . What does being Mexican really mean?" (67–68). Marcela, however, learns a valuable lesson about "being Mexican" when the date turns into a near-rape. As with Lupe's mother and gangbanger brother (Lupe is Marcela's only successful mentee), and several of the other poverty-stricken mentees we meet in chica lit books who seem to ultimately and often utterly reject the "better way" shown to them by better-off characters, the reader discovers along with Marcela that ethnic poverty seems almost to constitute a set of virtually intractable, *personal* character flaws, rather than exhibiting how larger structural problems exacerbate individual behaviors. As we will again see with Lauren and Amaury in *Dirty Girls on Top*, having a relationship with a Latino steeped in the "culture of poverty" is ultimately a dead-end street on the map to Latina Americanization.

Dirty Girls Social Club's Lauren seems to present the opposite scenario—she first dates Mexican American Ed *because* he "didn't complain about oppression and imperialism all the time. He was the first Chicano I'd known who had zero interest in lowriders or big graffiti murals" (140). Only after she breaks it off with Ed does she, like Marcela, test the limits of her distaste for an ethnic culture of poverty by having an affair with Amaury. He is a poor (but as Lauren thinks, at least in the first book, articulate) Afro-Dominican who must deal drugs to support his family: "I tell [the girlfriends] about my increasing curiosity in the kind of dangerous prettyboy tigres that roam the streets. . . . I tell them of my dream of saving one of them, making him a professional" (36). Lauren indeed helps to "save" Amaury, who by the end of the novel is on his way to professional success.

The language of uplift continues in *Dirty Girls on Top*, where Lauren also agrees to mentor a young, poor Latina. Unfortunately, we learn quickly that the work of "uplift" is not as uplifting as it might seem, since with poor Latinos/as, there is always the danger of an ungrateful relapse back into "old" ways and habits. Lauren admits that her experience with her first mentee, Shanequa, didn't go so well: "I lost touch with Shanequa four years ago, after she had her first baby at fourteen and decided to move in with her much-older drug-dealing boyfriend. I couldn't take the disappointment I felt around her" (197). In the same book, her next mentee, a young Dominican girl named Marileysis, is not only beautiful but looks up to Lauren as a role model, since she too wants to be a journalist. Though Lauren ungraciously feels Marileysis might surpass her at some point, she agrees to the relationship. After all, her salvation of Amaury seems to be working fabulously well, as we see when Amaury drives Lauren to the airport "in his black Lincoln Navigator with the tinted windows . . . with the new Vuitton luggage he bought me. . . . He wears his work clothes—trendy dark jeans from Express Men's, and a FUBU shirt with several large gold chains and colorful Santería beads around his neck. He is the new East Coast regional director of street teams and MySpace publicity campaigns for Wagner Records' Latin Division" (17). Yet despite the plethora of soothing real and near-real brand names, storm clouds are on the horizon. Although Valdes's first novel presented Amaury as "educated" in Spanish, literate in authors Lauren's never hoped to read in their native language, by the second book we understand that once again, you can take the Dominican out of the ghetto, but you can't take the ghetto out of the Dominican. As Lauren hears Puerto Rican Joe Segura speak Spanish, she realizes that Joe's Spanish sounds *"educated.* I am now getting fluent enough to tell that my boyfriend and I sound like country bumpkins when we speak Spanish, because I learned it from him and he's a hick and a hood, in Spanish" (195). Indeed as Lauren suspects, Amaury is carrying on an affair, with a beautiful teenage Latina-from-the-hood who—gasp!—is actually Marileysis, Lauren's new mentee (Lauren finds this out by browsing Marileysis's Facebook page). When confronted, Amaury informs Lauren that Marileysis herself is fine with him having more than one lover. When that approach doesn't work, Amaury regresses to his Dominican barrio upbringing so far as to try to rape Lauren, in something of the same way Marcela's date with the *vato loco* ends in an almost-rape. Amaury is gone from Lauren's life, and the book never mentions Marileysis again.

Usnavys, along with Shanequa, Marileysis, Amaury, and, in Rios's novels, Armando, Lupe Perez's mother and brother, and Lupe Perez herself, are iconic characters in chica lit. Shanequa, Marileysis, Armando, Lupe's mother and brother, and Amaury represent those whose somehow innate class deficiencies and "cultural" (in)ability to truly move on up indicate certain things especially to the Latina reader. These characters teach the chica heroine, and not coincidentally the reader, that a coming of age into material and ethnic American success for women must be achieved by asserting, by way of violent rejection, a presumed culture of ethnic poverty from which these other characters ultimately cannot move. It is important to understand that in these books' didactic zeal, the assertion of an intractable ethnic poverty is just as important as the scenarios of its rejection. Teaching the same lesson from the other side, then, Valdes's Usnavys and Rios's Lupe Perez, with their climb up from poverty and their subsequent, though always difficult, transformation into middle-class cultural citizens, demonstrate the "doing" of Americanization to the Latina reader.

In chica lit, the rejection of poverty as a culture of ethnic failure is the flip side of the non-ghetto character's relative ease at achieving material success. Yet again, the romance as well as career girl formulae of these novels means that the very material independence that chica lit's characters often take for granted is simultaneously presented as that which raises fears that if they are too successful, they will never find the right man. As Philips again points out, "Despite their assertions of the right to a career and independent income, there is a very traditional fantasy of femininity in these novels" (Philips 247–48). As the main character Tamara in *Hot Tamara* says to Will, whom she has discovered is the correct man for her, "'I want to stay here in LA. And I want to live together in this house with you.' . . . There, she said it. And lightning didn't strike. Feminists didn't storm the house" (Castillo 245). In chica lit, genre formulae, the identification and rejection of an assumed ethnic culture of poverty, and the privileging of a consumer persona all attempt to reconcile and smooth over the tensions inherent in contemporary US culture's "material contradictions in the expectations of femininity" (Philips 249).

Indeed, another aspect of the discourse around class in these novels lies precisely in the fact that chica lit novels depend on genre elements that have developed to assume a heroine with, no matter her possibly humble beginnings, un(re)marked white privilege and the access to resources which whiteness can bring. Chica lit's strategy of combining genres, while necessary in order to address the complexities of how to assign material success to characters whose embodiment is not just raced and classed but gendered, nevertheless encounters problems in inserting its characters into middle-class whiteness.[3] Thus in chica lit, which often foregrounds inherited ethnicity over race, the chica heroine's "color" is also often unmarked or if remarked upon, not connected with structural racism or sexism. Thus most chica lit heroines are often what I think of as "unmarked ethnic" women, whose (non)color allows their insertion into the genre requirements usually only inhabitable by white women, and presented as simultaneous with "being American."

Yet even those chica lit characters presumably not personally interested in making money, even voicing concerns about class difference—such as Marta Acosta's heroine Milagro—have, as Lauren puts it in her description of Usnavys, "no problem getting men" (12). Women's independence has long been understood as not enough for her fulfillment in life either emotionally and, at a time of "flexible accumulation," financially. In this way, representations of the heroine's independence from romantic entanglements not only threaten the social order but also raise the specter of her financial, if not emotional, failure. That a woman is not "complete" without coupledom is part of the traditional "fantasy of femininity" of the romance, indeed is one of its conventions. Yet chica lit lifts this convention almost entirely and uncritically sutures it onto assertions of the heroine's individual abilities, with the result that cultural and classed imaginaries—presented as mirroring not just the fantasies but the realities of Latinas—of what it means to be both Latina and American, successful and romantically coupled, often sit uncomfortably together.

Mexican Kitsch

In narratives that emphasize the primacy of the self-made ethnic woman (with a little help from her friends), her "style" often helps to construct the heroine's subjectivity; that is, the chica's taste in clothes, accessories, makeup, and hair sometimes constitutes, for the experienced reader of popular women's fiction, a shorthand for understanding that character's true self. Especially for Mexican American authors the often popularly asserted danger of laziness and criminality represented by a seemingly inherent "Mexicanness" means handling a character's Mexican American style and/or taste gingerly.

Real-world Mexican (American) entrepreneurship can echo this problem. In 2007, the Mexican T-shirt company NaCo ("naco" is Mexican slang for "kitschy") gained footholds in the United States with small business owners as well as large department stores such as Macy's. Despite its successes, however, NaCo's experiences in the United States sounded a cautionary note about the dangers of evoking Mexican people's apparent racial difference from "whites." It is worth quoting extensively from Laurel Wentz's article in *Advertising Age* on the results of a Mexican American company's marketing of "Mexicanness" in the United States:

> When Marcos Hernandez, CEO of San Antonio shop FPO, signed on his latest client, he enthusiastically immersed himself in its world . . . raiding his mother's house for Hispanic-kitsch touches—a great-grandmother's photo, a picture of "The Last Supper," an image of the Virgin of Guadalupe. It was just the right atmosphere for NaCo, a trendy Mexican apparel company trying to break into the US Hispanic market with a mix of irreverent messages that appeal

to emotions ranging from self-mockery to nostalgia. In Mexican Spanish, *naco* is a derogatory slang term for lower-class tackiness, but NaCo has reinterpreted it as an inside joke that treats kitsch as cool. . . . NaCo got its first US break with a national retailer last week when 17 Macy's stores in Texas and Atlanta began stocking eight women's $25 T-shirts . . . Macy's, however, quickly found that not everyone is amused by NaCo's sense of humor. Its T-shirt with the fashion-parody slogan "Brown is the new white" drew immediate fire from a conservative anti-immigration website, generating e-mails to Macy's threatening a boycott and online rants about racism and immigrants trying to take over America (one poster pointed out a possible link between Macys' red-star logo and communism). Fox News did a story, and Macy's pulled the "Brown is the new white" shirt. (Wentz np)

In the case of group responses to NaCo's "Brown is the New White" T-shirt, and corporate decisions made in the face of such responses, it is clear that even a coolly ironic, fun, or "kitschy" sense of style has its social limits. Bourdieu reminds us that taste functions as a "social orientation" within those spaces where there is a close "correspondence between goods and groups." This is of paramount importance in fiction where proper gendered behavior includes a sense of class and ethnicity (two ineluctably interwoven, though heavily contested, areas) as inevitably bound not so much to a family or community background but instead to consumer practices:

Taste is a practical mastery of distributions which makes it possible to sense or intuit what is likely (or unlikely) to befall—and therefore to befit—an individual occupying a given position in social space. It functions as a sort of social orientation, a "sense of one's place," guiding the occupants of a given place in social space towards the social positions adjusted to their properties, and towards the practices or goods which befit the occupants of that position. It implies a practical anticipation of what the social meaning and value of the chosen practice or thing will probably be, given their distribution in social space and the practical knowledge the other agents have of the correspondence between goods and groups. (466)

In the case of representing Mexicanness or Mexican Americans in the United States, Mexican "style" can go either way: particularly for the representation of Mexican American characters, I argue, evoking a kitsch sentimentality for the culture of a tourist Mexico can lessen, in the mind of the reader, the perceived danger of the "real" Mexico.

If "culture" in a commodified, neoliberal economy has become a "well-known instrument of entrepreneurship used by . . . business" (Dávila, *Latinos, Inc* 9), the very marketability of chica lit itself—its own publishing success—is bound up with its heroines' learning how to Latinize their presumed cultural heritage so that it fits into the American dream. Notwithstanding the marketing of a multicultural America, once broached, the very question of what a Latina in America should look like generates fuzzy and ambiguous answers, weighted down by contradictory imaginings about cultural and legal enfranchisement. In the face of such ambiguity, genre constraints and marketplace demands pull chica lit back from the necessarily incoherent realities of an immigrant/slave/indigenous United States so as to present a clearer, more hierarchical national order.

As Morrison notes, "attempts to construct a market-friendly Latinidad result in the misrepresentation and sometimes erasure of specific regional and national origin groups. . . . Mexican Americans often fare the worst in terms of stereotyping and marginality within the mass media. . . . The explanation . . . lies at the intersection of the profit logic of capitalism and a broader cultural and racial logic in the United States that places Mexicanos on society's lowest rungs, rigidly fixed in the mainstream cultural imagination as low-class laborers, interloping immigrants and unassimilated aliens" (310). As we have seen in my discussion of the character of Amber/Cuicatl, invidious comparisons with Mexican or Mexican American poverty often instruct the readers of chica lit such as Valdes's novels on how material success enables a commodified, stylish cultural citizenship—across the myriad differences between, say, an Afro–Puerto Rican Usnavys and a Jewish Cuban Sara. As Dávila has shown, marketers of commodified "Latino" food or home goods engage the public in an imaginary ethnic subject who is conservative and family-oriented, and who values hard work, in part to "correct" the other side of the coin, the popular imaginings of Mexicans as dirty, lazy, and illegal. The entertainment industry in particular, and its related industries in popular publishing, has embraced a US imaginary of the urban, "hot, sexy" Latino/a rather than the down-market and possibly immigrant Mexican, clutching her belongings in plastic grocery bags (Valdes, *Dirty Girls* 7). Thus, to be perceived as a (brown) "Mexican" can conjure up a myriad of seemingly paradoxical notions. As we have seen, certain Mexican images and objects—mostly those connected with folk or popular culture, such as the Cinco de Mayo and Día de los Muertos holidays, or *milagros* charms and *lotería* images—have now become part of a US kitsch sensibility. This is especially true when they are coupled with an evocation of a nostalgia for an imagined time, especially from the early half of the twentieth century, when "Mexico" meant vacations and siestas and an exotic, ancient, and colorful "culture" just right for a too-mechanized United States.

In this sense the novels and how-to crafts books I examine in this chapter depend on a long tradition of US imaginings (not to say Mexican state promotions) of a Mexican style that recovers the sentimental kitsch value of cheap and colorful mass production. Here, "class work can be seen to continue unabated in relation to kitsch" (Potts 4). Maribel Álvarez's *Made in Mexico* shows how

> In the symbolic context of relationships born out of colonial encounters, the word "colorful" evokes shades of inequality—a veiled reference to the unconscious pleasures often associated with childish things, carnival and exuberance, loud laughter, outdoor markets, or people once considered "without culture" yet caught in the quagmire of "too much culture." Colorful is an adjective that stands in contrast to the opacity of a more developed nation. . . . The perception of Mexico as a place "overwhelmingly visual" that possesses "an innate aesthetic sensibility" has fueled the construction of a romantic primitivism about the people and the objects of this [seemingly] enigmatic country. (18)

As John Harner also notes, "Popular art, especially indigenous art, has been . . . promoted by the Mexican government since 1921. . . . The attraction of American consumers to Mexican folk art began with a flourishing of cultural interaction between the two countries in the 1920s. . . . [V]ernacular goods give American consumers the exotic feeling of Mexican material folk culture, a taste of Mexico that they can bring home" (355). Mexican American chica lit authors in particular must attempt to manage the unruly assumptions that govern US "class work" around the notions of what it means to be Mexican American. The nostalgic desires conjured by a "taste of Mexico" allow Mexican American chicas to safely engage with an imagined Mexico as a design and decorative resource for their self-presentation as culturally American. Images of Mexican culture might be "stereotypical," as both Star and Lauren complain of piñatas and Mexican jumping beans. Yet Star's apparently inherent connection to Mexican style, once acknowledged, can be leveraged into a personal style, a source of sentimental and romantic pleasure and, eventually, an income.

Kathy Cano-Murillo's craft books as well as her "Crafty Chica" novel series are linked to her extensive *Crafty Chica* blog. Her own (re) discovery of what it means to be Mexican is an imagined combination of colorful peasant and folk art that can be "respectfully reinvented for the sake of décor" (*Casa Loca* 13). To a greater extent than Acosta, Cano-Murillo engages with the idea that the "bad taste" of Mexican working-class culture—as revealed in its cheaply handmade objects and colorful, sometimes outlandish folk and religious images—can be, for the Mexican American chica, a fun connection to a more exotic and flamboyant décor and personality. This avoids the more egregious, open distaste for the ways in which "Mexico" conjures up, in the work of authors like Valdes and Rios, representations of poverty, lowriders, class and ethnic resentment, gangbangers, general criminality, and a desire to shave Frida Kahlo's unibrow right off. For both Acosta and Cano-Murillo, taste—in clothes, makeup, décor, and accessories—comes to stand in for a nostalgic, personal, and domesticated sense of a largely imagined Mexican cultural heritage with a presumed affinity for, as Cano-Murillo says, the "rustic, shiny, colorful, exotic . . . dramatic, flamboyant" nature of "Latin" style (*Casa Loca* 12).

Cano-Murillo writes the most overt representations of kitschy Mexican American ethnicity through her direct engagement with a sense of Mexican taste as a fun and funky heritage. Cano-Murillo begins her *La Casa Loca: 45 Funky Craft Projects for Decorating and Entertaining* (2003) by openly confessing her own early, assimilated American tastes and lack of Mexicanization: "Aside from eating my dad's tamales every Christmas, I never had the desire to indulge in anything related to my culture. . . . I giggled when I confessed [to her *vato loco* date, now her husband] that I had never so much as tasted a taco. He shook his head in shame when I confessed I'd rather be caught singing in the shower than listening to mariachis. . . . As it turns out, it was May fifth [Cinco de Mayo]" (8). As guided by her new *vato* boyfriend, she explores her new world of Mexican American culture, "My exuberant passion exploded into multicolored glitter! Viva! [sic]. . . . my husband and I have designed what we call Chicano folk art. . . . We are most happy when we can add spicy visual flavor to anything we can" (9). Continuing in this vein, Cano-Murillo writes,

> Ay Díos mío! How can one accurately define Latino style? . . . What it does happen to be is any or all of the following: diverse, rustic, shiny, colorful, exotic . . . dramatic, flamboyant . . . and so much more. . . . The best part is you don't even have to speak Spanish. Cubano, Mexicano, Puerto Rican, Nuyorican, Spanish, Chicano, Bolivian. . . . and so many other ethnicities can be mixed and matched to culturally converge under one vibrant umbrella. . . . romantic images from old world Europe to tribal scenes of Central and South America that are weighted with pre-Columbian influences. (12)

Here, ethnic style is evoked as a kind of pan-*latinidad*, a defining characteristic for Latinizing a cultural heritage that, for Cano-Murillo, can make you happy. At the same time, although Cano-Murillo is by no means a corporate Latina, she has commodified a rearticulation of "Mexican" culture into a US model of individual merit and economic entrepreneurship: and "the best part is you don't even have to speak Spanish." The kitsch sensibility of the entrepreneurial Mexican American heroine like Star or Milagro is translated into crafts, thrift-store finds, and over-the-top accessorizing. It becomes a knowing but also nostalgic evocation of the "bad taste" of working-class people, at the same time providing its producers with jobs and, in the case of Star, some fame and material well-being.

PARANORMAL MEXICAN KITSCH

At the very beginning of Marta Acosta's paranormal *Casa Dracula* series, Milagro de los Santos (punning is an integral part of Acosta's writing, so you'd better get used to it) finds herself in financial difficulties.

She muses, "You would think that a girl with a degree from a Fancy University would have been hired *muy rápido* by some big corporation. . . . All my attempts to become a worthwhile cog in the capitalist machine were met with rejection" (1). Her education has given her cultural capital in the form of a knowledge of literature, and even the ability to mock-speak in the seemingly stilted tones of bygone "literary" eras, as for example in this conversation with her best friend and FU graduate Nancy:

> "You never even finished *Pride and Prejudice*. I wrote that paper for you."
> "And now I am showing my tremendous appreciation for your scholarship. Also this gives you credibility with Anglophile aspirants, my little brown *amiga*." This is how we talked to each other. We thought being silly was the height of delightfulness. . . . [But] I worried that perhaps I, as a nonserious person, was only a beach read as well. I had just reread *Middlemarch*, and I had a deep and sincere desire to be a deep and sincere character. (4)

Yet although a degree in literature gives our heroine "class" and seriousness via cultural capital, in the "real" world of lowered job opportunities and romantic disappointments, Milagro tells us, "I'd become obsessed with finding the answer to my [romantic] misery in *Paradise Lost*. I'd received an A on my term paper, but my time would have been better spent getting advice from *Cosmopolitan*" (11). This rueful and slightly self-deprecating tone makes the book "relatable" to its readers, and at the same time leavens Milagro's disillusionments and hard lessons with humor.

In fact, being Mexican American rests not only on the ways in which there is a light sprinkling of Milagro's humorously portrayed political awareness of prejudice throughout each book. Even more importantly, the reader comes to understand that Milagro's inherent Mexican Americanness dictates, to a large degree, the flamboyant kitschiness of her personal taste. In *Happy Hour at Casa Dracula*, Milagro aspires to the Frida Kahlo "look":

> A skinny chick behind the counter in elaborate Frida Kahlo garb said, "*Hola*." Her dark brown hair was braided into a crown on her

head, two caterpillar brows sat above huge dark eyes, and her lipstick was bright red. I was dying to run back to the ranch and pencil
in my eyebrows.

"*Hola*," I replied. "Great stuff."

"Thanks. I take a few trips a year to buy it," she said pleasantly with
no inflection. She was an assimilated Latina like me. (182)[4]

The tastes of Acosta's Milagro do not necessarily draw her only
to things Mexican—as we will see, by way of being an "assimilated
Latina," her tacky taste can draw from just about anywhere. However,
the fount of her kitsch sensibility lies in the ways her ethnicity impels
her desire to, for example, pencil in her eyebrows in imitation of Frida
Kahlo's unibrow. The novels' campy tone allows the reader to understand this while Milagro herself is self-deprecatingly earnest when
displaying her taste for all things tacky. For example, when we first
meet Milagro in *Happy Hour*, we learn she has an "affection for rock-
chick" looks and thrift-store finds (56), she loves tropical drinks "in a
coconut with little parasols" (19), she considers her rather zaftig Mexican figure "charming and decorative" (35), although her mother, who
is a social climber, does not consider Milagro's large chichis "tasteful."
As Milagro gets ready for a party, she decides that "some people were
just not meant to be demure. . . . I added more eye shadow and mas-
cara and lipstick" (190). By the time we get to *Bride*, Milagro's friend
Nancy uses Milagro's undemure style and affection for accessories as
a metaphor for ethnicity. She chides Milagro for her social conscience,
explicitly making a connection between her sense of ethnicity, class,
and sensitivity to racism: "Mil, you mix up patriotism for bigotry.
You're always hyper-sensitive like there's this big conspiracy or something, and you know how I adore your whole ethnic thing, but let's not
overaccessorize. Be a dear and pass me the new *Cosmo*" (327).

Because *Bride of Casa Dracula* is (presumably) the novel in which
Milagro finally gets married, this book in particular is preoccupied
with questions of whether or not to overaccessorize. On the one hand,
the novel links class, taste, and a certain liberal ideology around concerns with prejudice, via its unspoken connection between Milagro's
overaccessorizing as both metaphor and actual result of her sense of
Mexican ethnicity. On the other hand, the romance formula is never
clearer than in this particular book of the four. It forces the wedding/

comedy of manners plot to link taste to questions of social inequity. At the same time, it deposits all the signs of "high" class, wealth, and privilege on the side of the (white) vampires who nevertheless are themselves persecuted for their blood. Although Milagro is closely allied, through romantic ties, with these privileged-but-persecuted people, the novel, like the two previous ones, continues to insist that she is not, ideologically speaking, invested in their wealth or even their class status: "Oswald had booked a room for me at his favorite hotel, a posh place smack in the heart of things, and insisted on paying for it. I could ponder my discomfort with our vastly different economic circumstances while I soaked in the marble Jacuzzi" (48). As we have seen earlier, through the traditional fantasy of a love which overpowers and renders one helpless in its grip, Milagro can—indeed, must!—enjoy the fruits of privilege at the same time that she can hold to a distrust of class difference.

Bride mirrors the ways popular culture has elevated and commodified weddings and wedding planning—from breathlessly over-the-top magazine and tabloid coverage of celebrity and royalty weddings to television reality shows such as *Say Yes to the Dress* and *Four Weddings*. Here, weddings and their more or less tasteful planning not only stand in for ideological questions of class but also, because it is assumed that wedding planning is a woman's task, function as a way to instruct women in questions of consumerism, status, and even race. (This is also true of the heavily commodified wedding industry in United States. TLC's *Four Weddings*, for example, has several times pitted one black woman's "culturally different" wedding—she will sing with or to her beloved at the altar, or the groomsmen will perform a dance in the midst of the wedding, or rap and hip-hop music will feature prominently at the reception—against three other white women's more "normal" wedding plans.)

We as readers know through much foreshadowing that Oswald is in fact not the perfect man for Milagro. Thus, her discomfort with the family wedding plans can hint at the unsuitability of the match, while it also shows that her innate but lovable tackiness makes her uncomfortable with "serious" taste, via her contrasting notion of "style." When Milagro complains, "Oswald's mother thinks [the wedding] will be a nightmarish carnival of mariachis, chili pepper-string lights, and taco table, and I'll wear a gown made of purple polyester lace.

Why does she think I'm tacky?" we as readers know, of course, why: she's "ethnic." Yet Nancy replies soothingly, "You're a lavish girl, and people mistake subtlety for style, when it is no such thing. I'm developing an entire thesis around this. Chapter titles will tell you what *isn't* style, such as 'Monochromaticism isn't Style'" (37). Here, Nancy assures Milagro that her "lavishness," understood as ethnic unsubtlety, is indeed style, a term which tends to evacuate the more ideologically-loaded "taste" so that social and class distinctions can become merely personal ways of design, décor, and fashion style, rather than pointing to questions of inequality.

Again, when Oswald has the "favorite family department store" opened just for them to pick out wedding patterns, Milagro as a "lavish girl" (read: ethnic chica) is overwhelmed by all the expensive, refined, and "classic" items in the store. In response, she begins to feel an "off-balance, giddy sensation that I was about to break something very expensive" (16). Just when the tasteful plate patterns—all of them white—begin to seem the same to her, Milagro's eye is "drawn to a cabinet that held a glossy red plate with a leopard-print rim in black and gold. . . . I could paint my nails exactly the same shade as the plates and have my friends to tea" (17–18).

The tackiness of Milagro's vision, parodying the formality of Oswald's uptight family, at first seems to resonate with the character of Tamara in Mary Castillo's *Hot Tamara*. We first meet Tamara as she contemplates her freedom from her family's desire that she marry the boy next door. She discovers that her period has come while "Sitting in her Tía Yolanda's bathroom with goose-head faucets, antacid green walls, and pink towels with mermaids that looked like drag queens in shell bras" (1). However, *Hot Tamara* will transform her ethnicity via a valorization of artistic sensibility that overtly rejects working-class ethnic kitsch.

In *Hot Tamara* (the paperback cover of which asks, "What's life without a little spice?"), Tamara Contreras lives in a small town about two hours away from Los Angeles. She longs to get away from her Mexican American family and their distinctly Mexican American, working-class ideas (her father is a mechanic; her mother teaches at the local school) of proper decorating (tacky) and proper behavior for women. They—most especially her mother—want her to give up her ideas of graduate school, marry her conservative, straight-arrow

Mexican American childhood sweetheart, and teach at the local high school. She is also required to serve her younger brother at the table, and her family assumes that she will help put him through business school. Here, again, in something like the same move as is made in Acosta's books, the book's emphasis on taste and accomplishment tries not to be as rooted in naked consumerism as other chica lit fiction such as Valdes's. In fact, Tamara doesn't mind being situationally "poor" while she tries to get started on her dream, which is to own a gallery. The narrative instead depends on Tamara's rejection of the working-class notions of success held by her overly ethnic family, neatly summed up by her grandmother: Tamara tells the readers that being monolingual "was her Nana Rosa's fault. . . . who insisted . . . that the family was *New* Mexican. *No somos Méxicanos. You don't want them to be like those Mexicans who don't realize they're in America*, her abuelita would advise Mom while her cigarette spit ash onto the urine yellow shag carpet" (5). Yet Tamara makes no effort to try to learn Spanish; in some ways like her grandmother, Tamara does not in fact want to become more Mexican.

This novel is, instead, at heart a rejection of a certain kind of ethnic, working-class imaginary about what the signs of a US middleclass success are. This rejection is then set against a more bohemian aspiration for the signs of artistic—though still slightly ethnic—cultural capital. As *ranchera* music plays in the backyard, her mother and boyfriend speak Spanish so she won't understand what they're saying. Tamara represents the generation that has been encouraged to assimilate into mainstream America while staying close to the family, an always tricky combination often signaled by that generation's inability to speak Spanish. Although they are plenty "ethnic," it is the signs of a certain class capital that Tamara's Mexican American family lacks, and that they constantly though mistakenly pursue. The narrative drops clues to the family's aspirations as well as to their true socioeconomic class throughout the novel, from the Tiffany bracelets Tamara's mother wears even while cooking, to the dining room table "that was reported to have traveled across the Atlantic with their Spanish ancestors. But when Tamara had looked, she saw the Sears Roebuck warranty tag stapled on the bottom" (51).

In novels such as these, where class aspirations and the meanings assigned to cultural capital clash, as Philips notes it is often the romantic character's "style" credentials that signal to the reader, if not at first to the main character, who the final "correct" romantic choice will be: "The hero and heroine's partnership is destined in an alliance of shared tastes" (243). Thus, for Tamara a successful ethnic identity will ultimately be arrived at via her romantic liaison with Will Contreras, a Mexican American, barrio-born former Marine and firefighter who is also, as it happens, an artist. When Will (who has nursed a secret love for Tamara for years) learns she wants to be a gallery owner, he muses, "Never in a million years would he have believed he and Tamara Contreras shared something in common" (29). In spite of this sign of their future destiny together, the romantic obstacle is again, at least in Will's mind, his own (former) class status: growing up, "he lived in a foster home and his mom was a drug addict and his dad was doing thirty at San Quentin" (30). Yet his move "out of the ghetto" and into the Marines and firefighting converts Will's unfortunate origins and parentage first into romantic capital, then into cultural capital through his artistic talent, and ultimately into financial success when his paintings begin to sell. Such a move ensures that however damaged by the barrio's presumed culture of poverty, his masculine prerogative to a higher economic status than his mate is restored and indeed takes priority (his paintings sell at the gallery where Tamara serves, as she somewhat ruefully puts it, as a "glorified secretary").

As we have seen before, Will, Amaury, Armando (Marcela's *vato loco*), and Lupe Perez are, like the *Dirty Girls* barrio-raised, Afro–Puerto Rican Usnavys (named after a US military carrier), characters whose "movin' on up" class desires—or lack of them, like Armando the *vato loco* and Lupe's Mexican mother—indicate certain things to the reader. These characters teach her that achieving a coming of age into material and ethnic success for women is set against the presumed reality of a "culture" of poverty as well as in opposition to the misplaced taste and class aspirations of the stiflingly ethnic, working-class family.

This rejection calls for the substitution of a more modern, often urban, ethnic coupledom. For example, *Hot Tamara* evokes Will Contreras's ethnicity mostly through his Spanish surname, his paintings of his time in the barrio, and his adopted *abuelita*, Señora Allende.

Despite his barrio upbringing, however, he is now a successful artist and Señora Allende deeds her house to him as "the son she'd never had." Deborah Philips points out that in novels like these, "the women characters express an expectation that [they] be treated equally, while denying that there is any political dimension to that demand" (247–48). Such denial takes on a twofold dimension in chica lit: on the one hand, the right to a certain amount of independence is taken for granted without any discussion of the ways women have worked to overcome structural gendered ethnic and racial oppression. The relative ease—even for characters like Milagro and Tamara—with which these characters eventually effect, or sometimes literally fall into, class mobility denies how generational poverty and structural inequality renders such mobility a slippery, two-way street.

Chapter 3

Latinization and Authenticity

Now is a good time to finally state publicly how fucking annoying
it has been to read criticism of FilthyWomenDoGood that accuses
me of "creating stereotypes" in the characters of BoriBoricua and
Teodoro. These were thinly veiled portrayals of . . . people who I
loved a lot who were central to my life in City Y in the mid-1990s.
It was my life fucking story. So to all those idiots who said "That
pampered rich LatinCountry woman (as if!) is writing ghetto
Puerto Ricans and Dominicans because she's prejudiced and
thinks in stereotypes": Shut the fuck up.

—VALDES, *PUTA: AN EROTIC NOVEL*

In the United States, the notion that ethnicity is not natural goes
against what many people imagine as almost genetically inherent
"ethnic" markers, such as certain behaviors, the love for certain foods,
and even the expression of values. In this sense, Valdes offers an un-
beatable answer to her critics: her characters are not stereotypes because they are descriptions of actual, ethnic people who, presumably,
act in actual ethnic ways. Because the popularity of chica lit titles is
heavily author-dependent—that is, readers become extremely loyal to
specific authors—it is important to take into consideration authors'
own beliefs about the actual nature of "being Latina." In the first part
of this chapter, then, I look at how discourses of Latino "roots" and
"heritage" are important in the Latinization and selling of authors and
their books as authentically ethnic yet culturally American, and how
each biography and many interviews with the authors usually make a
careful point to emphasize it. Yet publishers and the public alike often
seem to have only vague and often contradictory notions about what
might comprise the combination of an American cultural enfran-

chisement with a Latina identity. Thus, I go on to identify the ways that chica lit's didactic or prescriptive orientation attempts to clarify both what ethnicity looks like and how to "Latinize" US cultural citizenship, thereby leveraging being Latina into a fully American adulthood for their chica heroines.

A Greater Connection to Her Roots

In this section, I devote time to discussing specifically how US Latinos/as are marketed, as opposed to the ways they are often portrayed in popular discourses about an invading tide of Latinos, "uniformly brown of face," as Valdes's Lauren puts it. Marketing—especially in the music, entertainment, and publishing industries—often depends on finding ways to "Latinize" American citizens who have Latin American or Caribbean heritage. "Latinizing" is a somewhat contested term that scholars such as Arlene Dávila and Agustín Láo-Montes identify in two different ways—on the one hand as the ways, historically and culturally, that Latino/a presence is woven into the very fabric of the United States, and on the other hand, as a policy or marketing emphasis on a cultural Latino difference that nevertheless does not threaten the presumed integrity of US cultural hegemony. For example, the publishing industry's Latinization of its authors often makes itself felt in an emphasis on authors knowing—or coming to know—their own "Hispanic roots." Yet such an emphasis poses something of a double bind. Although the books and their authors achieve success specifically because they are presumably "Latina," at the same time, as we have seen, the market demographic is clearly thought to be middle-class, assimilated women who themselves are ambivalent about what being "Latina" really means. For instance, shortly after the release of her second book, *Playing with Boys*, Valdes voiced what would become her standard response to assumptions made about her as an "ethnic" writer. In an interview with Lilia O'Hara for the *San Diego Union-Tribune*, Valdes, "(who doesn't speak Spanish) explains that her novels deal with people who have Latino roots but don't adhere to ethnic preconceptions. . . . Putting those feelings down on paper 'was revolutionary in the publishing world, for better or worse. Since you were a Latina, everyone wanted you to write magical realism, they thought that if you had a Hispanic name, you had some sort of dead person in the closet that spoke to you and I can't relate to those books'" (O'Hara F-1). As we can see here, then, publishers' insistence on, and Valdes's and others' rejections of, a model of "authentic" ethnicity remain a problem. At the same time as they might insist on their characters' *latinidad*, chica lit authors complain of feeling alienated by such public and publishing expectations. In O'Hara's interview, Valdes says of well-known Latina authors Sandra Cisneros and Julia Álvarez that she "didn't feel that the experiences in those books were my experiences. . . . [T]here's a sadness in those pages, an ethnic subconsciousness that I can't tune into" (O'Hara np). Here, Valdes articulates an undoubtedly genuine experiential difference— one that underscores her own desires for class status as well—which she then interprets as both a generational and, even more important, a somehow "unconscious" distance from those Latinas who write "magical realism" and speak to dead people (neither of which describes the kind of writing Cisneros or Álvarez actually does).

Yet on the other hand, chica lit authors also struggle with the notion that as Latinas, their own ethnicity is somehow inherent. A blog post from 2004 by *Crafty Chica* author Kathy Cano-Murillo pokes fun at expectations about what ethnicity means, especially for women, at the same time that she accepts the notion that an "ethnic" skill like making tamales is in the blood. "I'm a strong-willed woman, college educated, a multi-tasking queen. . . . But why can't I cook? This feeling of inadequacy hits me every December. As a Latina, aren't I supposed to be genetically engineered with culinary super powers? Geez, at least for tamale making season! My dad, uncle, nana, aunts and mom-in-law are all tamale maestros. You'd think I'd pick up a few tips." Mexican American author Mary Castillo notes in the back pages of her debut novel *Hot Tamara*, "In my family we didn't speak Spanish or even identify ourselves as Mexican. I was a fourth-generation American on my dad's side, who happened to be Mexican" (46). Yet in a blog entry from 2006 (the same year she published *In Between Men*), Castillo addressed head-on the question of speaking Spanish:

A few months ago when I was at the Catalina Magazine party in L.A., I met a really cool woman who is a marketing guru and pug mommy. Whenever I talk to someone whose first language is Spanish, I know that sooner or later they're going to hate me. Or, pity me. Frankly, I don't know which one is worse. No matter what we're talking about—cuisine, travel, books, people we work with—the conversation always boils down to The Question: "*¿Hablas español?*" I try to draw out the moment before I answer. There is a friendship at stake. But then I must answer no and the light in their eyes switches off and the conversation, no matter how engaging it had been, is over. (marycastillo.com)

Thinking about her fourteen-month-old son, Castillo goes on in the same post to note that he loves mariachi music. Thus, Castillo muses, "perhaps the spirit of Spanish is stronger than actual words. It is the umbilical cord that connects us to the revolutionaries, the conquistador[e]s, the Aztecs and the Mayans; it is rooted in and thrives from the soul. Am I a broken link in that history just because I rely on my trusty, *Making Friends in Mexico* to understand Spanish? Are my stories, my son a discontinuation of these people?" Her answer: "Nope. Nada de eso." Here as elsewhere a discourse of "roots" and "heritage" is not only important in the selling of chica lit books but also to underscore, however attenuated, the proper US Latinization of its authors.

Publishers and marketers often present ethnic producers and consumers as exotic yet homegrown. Speaking at least a smattering of Spanish (which usually disappears by the third generation, unless the family insists on it) and eating recognizable ethnic food becomes the "difference" we assume is somehow inherent to Latinas/os, and against which authors like Valdes continue to argue. Yet it is a difference absolutely necessary to market chica lit as distinct from, for example, chick lit. As Erin Hurt maintains in her incisive reading of *Dirty Girls Social Club*, "the chick lit genre . . . severely constrains [chica lit] cultural work. . . . The contradiction of the content's complex work of exploring and redefining identity and the genre's need to produce and sell the literary equivalent of cotton candy produces an ambivalent Latinidad that argues for a common American sameness, but also insists on a distinct ethnicity" (34). Thus Castillo's own musings on her inability to speak Spanish seem to turn on an essentializing discourse of a "blood" or "soul" link to Spanish and all it implies in a Mexican context (including, apparently, a connection to the Aztecs and Maya, who had Spanish forced on them). Having a presumed "blood" relationship with those who speak Spanish might be a good marketing narrative, but native fluency (or even an *accented* fluency in English) is often associated with being foreign. As an author of chica lit, Castillo must walk a fine line in denying that she is the "broken link" in some imagined "Hispanic" continuity between the time of the Conquest and a contemporary fourth-generation Mexican American life, yet making it clear that her Americanness is not tainted by a native or "foreign" fluency in Spanish.

The demands of Latinos and Chicanos in the 1970s (not to mention contemporary demands) were for greater ethnic autonomy, rights, and recognition of difference rather than overt disenfranchisement and invisibility. Several of the authors I examine—Valdes, Rios, and even Castillo—instead tend to reconstitute Americanization as the inclusiveness of a pluralistic nation where "a positive work ethic" is a main requirement for (ethnic) success (despite, as we will see, Valdes's brief but ultimately muffled critique of the "fantasy" of hard work as the way to the American dream). For example, Rios's April 2, 2009, blog entry includes her musings on the ongoing practice of deporting young, American-born Latinos to their parents' countries of origin: "I came across an interesting article called Deporting the American dream. . . . Curious, I read it, and found it was about the Salvadoran deportees, and their re-acculturation into Salvadoran society. . . . mostly the article talks about how they have taken American ways back to their country. . . . But what are these 'American ways'? A gang culture. Tattoos and hip hop. *This* is what they took back" ("What Is the American Dream?"). Rios continues, "Used to be that people would think of progress, and a positive work ethic when they thought of America. When my father would think about returning to Argentina . . . the things he knew he would miss were things like being able to get a job. . . . or having access to the newest and best technology." The nostalgia for bygone values intimated in this commentary ("used to be") functions in two ways: like Willy Loman, it gestures to an imagined American past of dreams fulfilled while it solidifies the ongoing and often internalized pressures on US Latinos for acceptance into a middle-class, assimilated status that carries with it a desire for the privileges (if not the actuality) of whiteness.

Latinizing Ethnicity, Making Americans

As Marta Caminero-Santangelo remarks in her essay on the term *latinidad*, "The meaning of 'latinidad,' ostensibly a fairly straightforward term that translates to 'Latinoness,' is actually quite fraught" (13). She notes that the label "implies questions of authenticity" as well as of difference and opposition. As she continues,

> While the idea that "Latino" contrasts with "Anglo-American" is regarded as fairly self-evident, what is less immediately obvious is that "Latino" also potentially contrasts with terms like "Chicana," "Cuban-American," or "Puerto Rican." . . . Chicanos have had a particularly fraught relationship with panethnic terms such as "Latino". . . While often treated as a synonym for "Mexican American" the term "Chicano" has strong connotations lacking in the hyphenated label: it suggests consciousness of—and politicization around—issues of oppression, racism, identity, and inequality; an anti-assimilationist attitude with regard to US culture; and a privileging of indigenous over Spanish colonial roots with regard to Mexican culture. (15–16)

Complicating the fact of inter-"Latino" differences across racial, class, national, and generational lines is the wobbly nature of what "Latino" means in the popular imagination. Prescriptions for Americanization have always advocated the loosening of ties to the country of origin. Yet at the same time, the relatively new discourse of multiculturalism focuses on the retention of such remnants from other cultures as can easily be incorporated into the nation's imagined sense of itself, such as foods (salsa), celebrations (Cinco de Mayo), and music and dance (salsa again!). Added to this is the increasing importance of marketing narratives about Latinos and their presumed impact on the culture of the States; celebratory campaigns assert that the influx of Latin and Caribbean Americans, still craving the tastes and sounds of their homelands, will change the way America eats (or dances, or celebrates holidays), indeed for the better.

Valdes's characters, while complaining of (and simultaneously informing the reader about) popular US ideas about Latinas, at the same time seem to celebrate the market as the place where Latinos will change America. Alexis, in Valdes's second book, *Playing With Boys*, complains,

> It had been *my* idea to give . . . [a] hefty donation to UCLA. I sug-

gested the gift as a way to raise [Los Chimpances del Norte's] visibility among mainstream Americans, and in the process raise the profile of all successful Mexicans and Meximericans here, which, in the end, might improve my life too. And who knew, maybe if L.A. powerbrokers started to see that we Messicans had money—*real* money—and not just, I dunno, pruning shears and toilet brushes, they might start to produce movies where the Mexican was a real person and not just a *gun*. (5–6)

Mexican American Alexis is an upwardly mobile young publicist for a Mexican musical group. She displays an apparently unshakeable faith in such marketplace narratives and their concomitant storyline that investing money in the marketplace (of ideas or of movies) not only will raise Mexican American visibility but will convince Hollywood that Mexicans and Mexican Americans should be portrayed to the rest of the nation as "real person[s]" and not just objects. (As in the 2001 movie *The Mexican*, starring Brad Pitt, where indeed "the Mexican" is a gun.)

Valdes's work provides some of the clearest examples of how marketing in particular takes the differences among Latinos born and/or raised in the United States—and already legally American—and "Latinizes" them into a general image of panethnic racial and cultural sameness. Lauren, the principal narrator in *Dirty Girls Social Club* and a columnist for a prominent Boston newspaper (*Sex and the City*'s Carrie Bradshaw's job comes to mind), comments on the "Hispanic" marketing bandwagon (the very one, the aware reader must realize, that has produced the book we are reading). Hired as the token Hispanic at her newspaper despite the fact that she doesn't speak Spanish, Lauren complains about already-inscribed racial perceptions of what Latinas are "supposed" to look like (brown). Her newspaper's advertisements for her column, placed on the sides of buses, misrepresent the fact that Lauren is white (half white Cuban exile on her father's side, half white Irish American "trailer trash" on her mother's side): "Money talks, see. Hispanics are no longer seen as a foreign unwashed menace taking over the public schools with that dirty little language of theirs; we are a domestic *market*. To be *marketed* to. Thus, me. My column. And my billboards. Greed makes people do crazy things. Craziest thing of all is the way the promotions department had my face *darkened* in the picture so I looked more like what they probably think a Latina is *supposed* to look like. You know, *brown*" (9). Alexis of *Playing With Boys*, on the other hand, is proud that Latinos are part of a "domestic market": "As I often had to tell reporters, America was changing, fast. Tortillas now outsold bagels. Famously, Americans now ate more salsa than ketchup. Wal-Mart carried plantains, yucca, and Goya products. Kraft in the United States had come out with something they called 'mayonesa,' a Mexican mayonnaise with lime. Why? Not because they were nice. Because they *had to*" (5). For a minute, it seems that Lauren and Alexis are on opposite sides of the debate: Are Latinos routinely misrepresented in the media, or have Latinos created important changes in American culture? As it turns out, both characters fundamentally agree. Again, in *Playing with Boys*, although Alexis seems to be stating that the consumption of tortillas, salsa, and mayonesa marks "cultural change" in the United States, her final words on the subject undermine the potentially frightening thought of "biculturalism." "Some academic types," Alexis asserts, "like my professors at Southern Methodist University, called people like me bicultural. But . . . I preferred to call it *American*" (5). Lauren muses to herself, "am I finally realizing I really ought to admit to what I am—a middle-class American—and stop trying to fit the foreigner stereotype loved by my editor?" While the reader might nod wisely over Lauren's self-knowledge, or chuckle at Alexis's mockery of clueless academics, we would miss the fact that what both Lauren and Alexis celebrate are corporate decisions to fold "ethnic" products into a marketing narrative about Latinos in America. Bits of culture, "Latinized" to conform to a multicultural sense of the United States as easily inclusive, are promoted in a US market not because, as Alexis says, the companies actually *have* to—she's right, it's not because they're nice—but because as Lauren notes in *Dirty Girls Social Club*, "money talks. . . . there's money to be made." What both Lauren and Alexis show us is that "America" is *not* changed—but that if Latin American products can be Latinized—that is, Americanized with a touch of something different—and can then make money, then salsa and tortillas can be as American as Mom and apple pie.[1]

As we have seen, in chica lit the use of Spanish is often evoked as an authentic marker of *latinidad* while its rejection is a marker of middle-class Americanization. Here, language retention rather than

food becomes the vexed site of questions about full cultural enfranchisement. Isa Avellan, the heroine of Castillo's *In Between Men*, is a
high school English as a Second Language (ESL) teacher. In this novel,
the character's Mexican *American* identity is not in question, since
she is located in a community of Californian Mexican Americans
who have lived in this small California town for generations. Actual
Spanish is not the central point of contention in the novel; although
the characters code-switch just enough to underscore their Mexican
American names, the question of being fluent in Spanish is instead
projected—under cover, so to speak—onto Isa's foreign-language students, only two of whom are identified as to their nation of origin:
Vietnam and Iran. This avoids having Isa deal with ESL students who
are Latin American immigrants, or the children of Mexican American migrant workers, working around the vexed question of bilingual
Spanish/English education in the United States.

As is often the case in chica lit, we are introduced to Isa on one
of her worst days; after divorce from a genuine asshole leaves her
with a son to raise, Isa has given up all thought of romantic success,
much less sexuality. Thus the book opens with the students voting,
Facebook-style, that she is the "least fuckable" teacher in the school,
while her former husband has agreed to go on a sexist talk show to
discuss in grim sexual detail why he and Isa broke up. To combat this
mountain of shit coming down on her, her *comadres* insist on giving
her a "makeover" before setting her up with a hotly handsome Mexican American man, Alex, whom she is convinced (without much reason) doesn't like her. To make matters worse, when she does go out
with him, it turns out he does find her "fuckable" and their sex is so
passionate they forget to use birth control: yep, you guessed it—Isa
gets pregnant, and spends the rest of the book in more or less amusing
romantic misunderstandings with the man of her dreams. All comes
together, he proves to be a man of worth through a steady job, and
proves himself a good potential parent by ultimately bonding with her
son from her previous marriage (after a rocky start). In spite of Isa's
initial resistance to his talk of getting married (she thinks he's doing
it only out of a sense of duty), she finally accepts and Isa, her son Andrew, and Alex spend the last few pages getting a family ultrasound.

One of the most interesting aspects of the book (which otherwise
reads much like a standard contemporary "single mom" romance),

however, is that Isa finds she is also in danger of losing her job as an ESL teacher at the local high school because of school board–directed budget cuts. Castillo's descriptions of Isa and her interactions with her students from other countries itself walks a fine line around debates about the Americanization of non-native English speakers. Having been told that her ESL classes are at the top of the list of cuts the board is considering, Isa says,

> "Don't they realize they could ruin the education of students?" But she already knew the answer. Many people thought of ESL as a throwaway program, an excuse for immigrants not to assimilate and not to become "American." And since the parents of these kids didn't speak English and often came from countries where they didn't speak to authority, they were left at the mercy of decisions made by people who didn't understand or really care about them. But she knew these kids. They had been ripped out of their culture into this bold, often confusing American one. She knew that unlike bored Spanish One students who needed a foreign language credit, these kids needed ESL to survive. (61)

Isa tells her ESL class that their classes may be cut, and she wants them to speak in front of the board. The students understandably react with dismay: "'How can what we say change their minds?' Daniel asked as the unofficial leader of the class. 'They want to care about the money.'" But, as Isa replies, "'their jobs are to listen to the people whose lives they will affect' . . . even though she knew how idealistic it sounded. . . . 'They want us to be something we're not,' Myrna protested. 'I don't sound American; I don't act like it or dress like it. I don't want to let go of who I am'" (97). This sole outburst of rebellion, however, is undercut when Khadija volunteers that the customers who shop at the computer store where her brother works won't let him help them, instead telling him he should "go home," comments other students have also heard (97–98). It is clear here that although sullen Myrna has the right of it, what matters—in the class as well as in the book's didactic purpose—is how to "Americanize" enough so that one gets on in life. Not "letting go of who you are"—if that means acting, dressing, or speaking differently—is at the very least unproductive if not actively un-American. We as readers are made to feel sympathetic with the students at the same time that we understand that Americanization is not only desirable but also inevitable unless one actually *wants* to be poor and uneducated, and that it is also a matter of one's individual desire to "work hard" with a dollop of help from a few committed teachers. This is not to say that Isa does not care about the students (she is, after all, the motherly type), but she believes in her mission to help them become "good citizens." Thus, she tells them with a dose of tough love, "You either give up or you stand up to them and make them hear you. . . . Your fate is up to you" (98).

Later, again, Isa tries to pep talk her students by reminding them why they came to "America": "Remember what I said about what it means to be here in America?" A student, Daniel, raises his hand and replies, "'You say—said,' he corrected himself. 'That it's about having freedom to ask what you want'" (203). With the help of Joan Collins, whose broad-shouldered specter appears to Isa whenever she needs some moral support (yes, dear reader, it's true), Isa gets all the students to promise they'll be at the board meeting to help make a plea for the ESL class. However, at the fateful meeting her painfully shy yet bright Muslim student Khadija is unable to take the podium, whereupon an Anglo parent whose daughter had gotten into trouble with Isa takes the floor instead: "He used those tired old arguments that 'in the old days' students integrated faster and became Americans. Isa fought the urge to roll her eyes. . . . How many immigrant students left school because they felt stupid and humiliated by a system that refused to transition them into a strange and sometimes aggressive culture?" (235). Will all be lost? Khadija finally reluctantly comes to the podium, and makes her speech: "I was afraid of America when I came here last year. . . . In Ms. Avellan's class, I learned more about my new country and see it as a great place where you can become whatever you want, and where someone will help you achieve your dreams if you work, study, and be a good citizen" (256). Khadija's speech wins the day, and Isa's classes are spared. Here as with other Mexican American authors, the push is not just for assimilation through language—one could learn perfect English yet resist complete accommodation—but for an Americanization that includes a desire for socioeconomic enfranchisement, framed in more liberal, progressive language. Against the Anglo father's desire to just throw non-native speakers into the deep end of a "strange and aggressive culture," the framing of the plight of non-native students in the United States through the caring eyes of maternal Isa seems to bespeak a kinder, gentler attitude toward the need for assimilation and language acquisition. However, ultimately both Isa the caring ESL teacher and the Anglo patriarch believe, though this may not be immediately clear to the "beach reader" of this fiction, in the same outcome: that assimilation is not only necessary but a one-way street. As Isa's student Myrna says, immigrants to the United States must, in effect, turn themselves inside out in order to become American, while white citizens may gain from immigrants a few new recipes, some salsa at the grocery store, a bit of Spanish, and some fiestas to celebrate (or not, as they wish).

In Between Men Latinizes its characters while adhering to the discourse of an Americanized multiculturalism. On the other hand, Castillo's next novel, *Switchcraft* (2007), walks a finer line between the more familiar and presumably generalizable chick lit situations its chica heroines find themselves in, and their more specific Latinization. This novel presents heroines who are more polished and urban than small-town Isa and who also have, or have had in the recent past, more upscale careers: Aggie owns a boutique, while her friend, though now a stay-at-home mom, formerly had a career that enabled her, as we will learn, to save over one hundred thousand dollars. Neither has a career or even major problems that could be identified as specifically "Latina." The question one might ask of this narrative, then, is how it is "Latina enough" to fit the chica lit publishing niche, while still teaching the lessons of cultural American citizenship. As we will see, Latinization may again be able to solve the problem.

Switchcraft begins with one of its main characters, Aggie, in a relatable though again not specifically Latina position: worried about the success of her clothing boutique, she has gotten drunk and slept with beautiful Kevin, her closest male friend, with whom up until now she'd enjoyed "the kind of intimacy old married couples have, without the cumbersome matrimonial ties" (1). Within the next two pages, the reader is introduced to Aggie's recently deceased mother, who, while lovable, was low class, which we understand through a shorthand involving the mother's "signature skunk-striped hair," "double-wide in the Keystone Trailer Park," and the fact that she died from a heart attack "in the parking lot of Wal-Mart" (2). We know, however, that Aggie has transcended this unfortunate beginning and become slim and stylish not only because she has a boutique but also because she drinks "green tea martinis," wears matching black lace underwear, and the night before The Mistake with Kevin was wearing a "Diane von Furstenberg wrap" (4). Nevertheless, Aggie's financial and romantic problems overwhelm her, and to make matters worse, she has "baby fever," is jealous of her stay-at-home mom and best friend Nely, and wishes she could talk to her own mother again.

Although we see Aggie's surname—Portrero—in the first sentence of the book, it is never mentioned again. In fact, it is not until the fifth page that there is a hint that Latina/o ethnicity might play a role in the narrative. Aggie has been reading a book called *The Seekers of the Dead*, written by "Guru Sauro," and has signed herself and Nely up for a "girls' weekend at the exclusive Ventana de Oro," where a "transcendental meditation ceremony" is said to help people talk to dead loved ones and even see the future (5). Indeed, Guru Sauro and his weekend meditation ceremonies at the Ventana de Oro provide the book with an ethnic context by gesturing toward the figure of the shaman Don Juan, from Carlos Castañeda's wholly fictional but astoundingly influential series of books from the 1970s about his mystical education in the Sonoran desert of Mexico. However, if the reader is not old enough to remember Castañeda's work, the casual, almost throwaway Spanish names in the narrative gesture toward the "Latino" culture of Southern California, where Aggie and Nely live, and where her friend Kevin has an "haute Mexican cuisine" restaurant called Sazón (Seasoning).

However, nowhere does the narrative specifically mark Aggie or Nely as recognizably ethnic beyond their unaccented surnames. Nely has "flawless pale skin, brandy-colored eyes, and black hair" (16), while Aggie has "bone-straight, caramel-colored hair. . . . her skin was dewy and her lips pouty pink." Each woman thinks the other has a near-perfect life. Nely lives in "a suburban mom's mecca of Old Navy, Target, Baja Fresh, and Starbucks," while Aggie and Kevin live in Golden Hill, where Victorian mansions have been converted into lawyers' offices (16, 22). The women drive Nissans, diet on Slimfast, monogram their purses, work out to Yoga Boogie tapes; Nely takes her daughter to Jamba Juice while Aggie sells Dita von Teese lingerie in her boutique, Whatever Lola Wants. Although such relentless brand naming may seem too much, this practice has been a staple of genre fiction in general since the 1980s. Here, style is reified as a class identity that, even if Aggie has to sell her Nissan and drive her mother's 1969 Dodge Charger (for a while), nevertheless appears to describe inherent personality traits as well as class hierarchies. Where are the "chicas" in this chica lit novel, where it seems the main thrust of its lessons involve showing middle-class, American thirty-something women how to find their own bliss?

In this book, the journey to proper Americanization is signaled not by an identity crisis on the part of the Latino/a characters, as in books like *Becoming Latina* or *Waking Up in the Land of Glitter*, but by the (attenuated) Latinization of their Americanness. Indeed, the characters of *Switchcraft* are presented right from the start as comfortably inhabiting their unquestioned cultural Americanness. Here, then, the chica lit novel traces a journey to successful cultural Americanness that has already been made but is threatened by the possible failure of the chica heroines to fully achieve adulthood and self-acceptance. Thus Latinization works to highlight—and sometimes even to rescue and shape, as in the case of events after Nely and Aggie's body switch and back again—its characters' successful maintenance of their American middle-class status. Indeed, Aggie, Nely, and Kevin's unmistakable Americanness is first foregrounded by the book's supporting characters' slightly too-accented ethnicity. Simona Mendoza, also known as "La Cacuy,"[2] is Nely's Catholic mother-in-law from hell: she lives with them, and for example insists that her granddaughter be baptized, "Or else she'll still have her *cuernos*—her horns from original sin" (10). Nely's husband Simon, a mestizo Mexican American cop, is described in terms of his Native American heritage: although he is characterized as a loving husband and father, the emphasis on his mixed race heritage is slightly unfortunate as he is described as having a "thuggish" glare to go with a "stoic Indian face, with the long nose that was ever so slightly wide at the nostrils and flat cheekbones . . . built to intimidate criminals and keep small children in line" (14). At the spa, the "guru" Sauro is pictured through Nely's eyes as even more stereotypically Mesoamerican: his "chiseled face, harsh in the light of the fire, radiated a leonine serenity," and with his "bronze skin," he appears as if he has just stepped out "of a painting of a Mayan warrior" (43). This mashup of secondary characters' ethnic features and the evocation of "Mexican" shamanic practices sketches a largely imagined Mexican heritage. In turn, these identities provide a kind of contact ethnicity (like a contact high, but different) for Aggie and Nely, one whose proximity does not affect their Americanness, but one that can provide them with tools for maintaining their middle-class Americanness in spite of conflicts and disillusionments. Thus, while in each other's bodies after the guru effects a sorcerous switch, Aggie becomes more responsible by having to mother Nely's daughter and stand up to La Cacuy, and Nely, in Aggie's body, finds that she can save Aggie's sagging business. The comedy of errors that follows Aggie's and Nely's body switch ends with a crazed stalker who triggers Aggie's brush with death. This device allows the women to switch bodies back again and, finally, triggers Aggie's and Kevin's mutual expressions of love. At the same time, Aggie and Nely become business partners.

Switchcraft works especially hard to make it clear that Aggie's and Nely's putative ethnicity has nothing to do with their financial circumstances at the beginning of the book (we are never vouchsafed an explanation for Aggie's trailer-park mother). Although Aggie's business is in trouble, she is by no means poor; even Simona's class status is assured, though again never explained, by the whiff of Estée Lauder Youth Dew perfume and her Anne Taylor Casual outfits (8–9). As a cop, Simon is rescued from blue-collar status mostly by the fact that he supports both his mother and Nely, as well as by his hotness quotient and his ability to protect women when they need it. Kevin is quite simply a well-off restaurateur. As it turns out, Kevin, with his curly hair of "antique gold" and surfer's tan (2), is the key to the book's Latinization of these characters' unquestioned cultural Americanness. This is a process that will both be unthreatening and ensure the proper behaviors needed to continue the chica heroines' shared status as middle-class Californians. Thus, our first real clue to Kevin's ethnicity does not appear until a flashback scene when Aggie remembers her first glimpse of him coming into her boutique to buy a pair of Dita von Teese stockings; when he comes back a few days later to return the stockings, he mistakenly leaves behind his American Express card, where we casually discover his name is Kevin Sanchez (35). Despite her initial suspicion that Kevin is buying the stockings for a girlfriend, their friendship begins when Aggie learns that the stockings were for Kevin's mother, ill with cancer.

It is through Kevin's vocation as a chef of "high style" Mexican food where we can best see how the foreign nature of Mexican ethnicity can profitably be Latinized so as to augment Americanness. Kevin's thoughts of Aggie, in fact, are more often than not triggered by thinking about, or preparing, Mexican food. At Sazón, preparing an *asado de bodas* or "wedding soup" for a friend about to propose, Kevin remembers how he learned this recipe at fourteen, in Jalisco, Mexico, from his grandfather. Even though Kevin doesn't speak Spanish and has been sent by his parents to Mexico to "straighten up," the "language" of food allows them to communicate: "his grandfather, the chef of the home, found a way to speak to Kevin by sharing all his culinary secrets. 'Make this for your bride on your wedding day,' his grandfather had said. 'And the soup has all the flavors of marriage. Spice for fire, tortilla from the earth, and broth will bind it together'" (178).[3] Beginning in the 1990s and accompanying the so-called "Latino explosion" of that time, the phenomenal success of fiction such as *Like Water for Chocolate*, both book and movie, has cemented the popular US imaginary's conflations of spicy seduction and passion with Mexican food: "Kevin ladled the broth, thick and glossy with corn tortillas, roasted garlic, ancho chiles, Mexican chocolate, and succulent pieces of pork bobbing under the surface. Remembering his grandfather's thick, strong fingers, he watched his own fingers deftly create a small garnish plate of *crema*, *queso fresco*, and pungent Mexican oregano. . . . Kevin kept the courses small, remembering how his grandfather said if he wanted to seduce a woman, never fill up her stomach" (178–79). By virtue of the fact that it can be reproduced outside of Mexico and its nature as a consumable, Mexican food's cultural signification as a Latinized product is safely available for American consumption. Through this process of Latinization the presumed passionate nature of Mexicans and their culture is rendered functional for a Stateside market: Mexican food, here elevated to the level of art by its passage through the male line and its incarnation in this novel as "haute cuisine," renders Kevin's ethnicity both unthreatening and profitable. Indeed, the last chapter, devoted almost entirely to Kevin and Simon, has Kevin catering his own wedding. Through Aggie and Kevin's union, the signification of food as culture, reiterated time and again in Americanization discourses, takes center place. Indeed, even Simon and Kevin, each too "manly" to be completely at ease with the other and still disturbed by the thought that Aggie and Nely had switched bodies, begin to bond over Kevin's description of the wedding food:

"*Panuchos* with fried egg, chicken in red sauce, and frijoles colados. . . . Sopitos with shrimp and chicken. . . . *Crepes de carjeta*, sopapillas" (281). Even if we don't know the Spanish, as readers we end with our mouths watering, understanding the ways in which successfully Latinized culture brings tasty bits of spice, seduction, and difference to the commodified normality of prosperous American lives.

If Castillo's books assume their main characters' Americanness from the beginning, how, then, to resolve the ambivalence some characters in other novels *themselves* apparently feel about "being" ethnic? Estrella Esteban (who eschews her Mexican heritage to the point of calling herself Star), the Mexican American heroine of Cano-Murillo's *Waking Up in the Land of Glitter* of 2010, at first refuses to have anything to do with her "heritage" (this is a semi-autobiographical portrait, as we already know, of the author's own adolescence): "Even though her parents owned one of the valley's top Mexican restaurants, Star nixed anything that didn't come between two slices of nine-grain bread. Not that she disliked Mexican food (she had yet to explore it), but as a second-generation Mexican-American, it irked her that people assumed she spoke Spanish, knew how to make tamales, and smashed piñatas at all her birthday parties. She didn't want to be lumped into those stereotypes. So she rebelled by distancing herself from her culture" (13). It will be the lure of romance, coupled with the desperation for a grown-up career that motivates Star to come closer to "her culture." Initially reluctant, she is introduced to her Mexican culture through food, prompted by hot, artistic Mexican American Theo: "That night, [her date] Theo told her she should be ashamed [of never tasting Mexican food], and coaxed . . . her into tasting a forkful of green chili. . . . he scooted close, held the fork to her curvy lips, and she melted inside. Not from the smell of the food, but from his presence. In one slo-mo bite, her life's outlook changed and she wanted more" (13–14). Although Cano-Murillo avoids the name branding of *Switchcraft*, it is clear that Star/Estrella is also middle-class in terms of family and goals, and like Castillo's characters, her problems at first glance seem completely American. Unlike Aggie, Nely, and Kevin—who never seem to feel the need to complain about stereotypes—Star/Estrella is pictured through details of her family, her friends and her surroundings as somehow more inhabited, so to speak, by her Mexican American heritage. Although we understand that characters as different as Aggie and Star must both learn to "grow up," *Waking Up* follows the more traditional ethnic coming-of-age form, where Star/Estrella is, despite her protests, much more fully immersed in a recognizably Mexican American community from whence she will, as is promised, grow toward a fully American adulthood, itself achieved by attaining romance and financial stability through the Latinization of her "heritage."

From the beginning of *Waking Up in the Land of Glitter* Star/Estrella is a bubbly chica with no follow-through; she lives at home with her parents and does publicity for their Mexican restaurant, but never finishes any project she starts, so that as we begin the book even her parents and her best friend Theo have reached the end of their patience with her. The reader also knows, although Star and Theo must not be able to admit it yet, that they are in love with each other, but neither wants a relationship before they become successful. Through a comedy of errors that begins the book, Star makes one clueless, horrible mistake after another. She must find a way to regain the love and esteem of Theo and her parents and become a functioning member of American society, a process that through the course of the book is mapped onto a largely imaginary sense of Mexican creativity.

Star must both accept and leverage her Mexican heritage through a process of turning crafting into artistic expression, and will finally (after a myriad of twists, turns, and side plots) attain artistic recognition through her "Joseph Cornell meets Frida Kahlo" boxes (47). To make these, she uses huge amounts of hot glue, affixing into Romeo y Julieta cigar boxes cutouts from "Mexican novella comics," red glitter, and Spanish expressions like "Te amo" written inside banners in the manner of Mexican folk *retablos* (evoking Frida Kahlo's work). The lesson here is to turn her potentially alienating (because both "stereotypical" and in actual public opinion potentially dangerous) heritage into a plus by becoming the kind of woman who is savvy at extracting economic value from it, thereby winning back the respect of her parents, opening her own craft business, becoming an artist, and getting engaged to Theo (himself by now also a sought-after artist). Although California and Arizona, where *Switchcraft* and *Waking Up* are respectively located, have long had no dearth of vexed political issues around questions of Mexican American ethnicity, these questions, if brought up at all, are tangential to these narratives. More importantly, connections with an actual Mexico, or to a resistant Mexican American identity, are safely relegated to an "old school" and slightly embarrassing past, much as Valdes does in her *Dirty Girls Social Club* novels. For example, although Star/Estrella's father at one time identified as a Chicano, it is clear that such a self-identification is now out of date: "She loved that her dad, Alfonso Ortega Esteban . . . was the classic Mexican-American machismo father figure—with a twist. After going through the Chicano Activist era with his parents in the seventies, and then on his own in the eighties and nineties, he took a trip to Jamaica in 2000 and fell in love with reggae music. Therefore, Star called him El Rasta Chicano" (59). The political implications of identifying as Chicano, and even the possible political implications of loving reggae, devolve into a New Age, "one love/one world outlook" (15). In the end, despite their differences, both Kevin's and Star's Mexican Americanness is a "heritage lite." Kevin's grandfather is, apparently, safely dead and gone, and Kevin would no more think of himself as "Chicano" than he would identify as a Martian. Despite her parents' ties to Mexican food and music, Star comes to appreciate Mexican food and to use Mexican "culture" for artistic success only, at first, via her romance with Theo. Although out of all the authors whose works I examine here Cano-Murillo is the only one willing to use the term "Chicana/o" in a positive way, nevertheless *chicanismo* becomes a matter of personal choice, a Latinized ethnic style made to fit an attenuated, and thus mostly unmarked, ethnicity. As we have seen, in every chica lit book the assertion of an American sensibility must take place within the borders of the United States. If a chica heroine ventures into Latin or South America, as with *Dirty Girls*'s Elizabeth, who returns to Colombia, her return to the United States will be swift and her push for Americanization unchanged. Thus neither Aggie, Nely, nor Star/Estrella considers actually going south of the border; although Kevin learns to cook in Mexico, it is not his choice: he was fourteen, and his parents made him go. Like Aggie and Nely, his ethnicity is so deracinated that Mexico, or a Mexican heritage, becomes on the one hand a matter of a few brief memories and on the other a means of successful cultural Americanness.

Conclusion

Not Even the Mexicans

Lauren. . . . said something about giving several months' notice
at her job, so that she could move to Mexico and write a novel. At
first? *M'ija*, at first I thought the bitch was joking because I told her
to move to a different neighborhood. In my world, doesn't anybody
in her right mind . . . leave her lucrative career as a rising star . . .
to start all over in a third-world country, okay? . . . Not even the
Mexicans want to stay in Mexico, okay?

      —ALISA VALDES-RODRIGUEZ, *DIRTY GIRLS ON TOP*

As we have begun to see, several scholars, in their readings of Valdes's *Dirty Girls* novels, have made clear the ways in which this chica
lit series has posited Chicana, or, even worse, "Mexican" as an abject subjectivity related, as Usnavys puts it above, to the unutterably
wretched third-world environs of Mexico itself. As Amanda Maria
Morrison puts it, "Keying in on both race and social class and the
ways in which the two are inextricably linked, Valdes-Rodriguez attempts in her first two novels to render Latinas and Latinidad pal-
atable to mainstream consumers, who she claims 'tend to be young,
educated, professional women who love clothes, apple martinis, and
sex' by playing off of a dominant cultural logic that places Mexican
Americans at the bottom of both Latinidad's national-origin hierarchy and the US's racial-ethnic and class hierarchy" (313). From
no mention at all in *Dirty Girls Social Club*, Mexico itself comes to
occupy a small but importantly conflicted (and largely imaginary)
space in the world of *Dirty Girls on Top*. Early on in the narrative,
when the *sucias* have gathered for their yearly get-together at a re-

sort in New Mexico, Usnavys has a tryst with an African American man, who asks her why she's speaking "Mexican." Usnavys's immediate negative reaction lets us know not just that she is offended that he doesn't realize she's Puerto Rican (though in *Dirty Girls Social Club* Lauren warns us: "Don't tell her she's dark, though. Even though her daddy was a Dominican, ebony as an olive in a Greek salad, her mother has from day one insisted that Usnavys is light, and forbids her from dating '*monos*.'" [13]), but that he has identified Spanish as "Mexican": "'What's a fine African-American woman doing talking Mexican?' and it was all I could do not to turn him around and drop-kick his ass. . . . 'For your information, I am Puerto *Rican*,' I told him . . . 'And the language you heard was *Spanish*. Ain't nobody in the world speak no *Mexican*, okay? Mexican? That's not a *language*, now shut your mouth before you start to look ugly to me'" (9). Mexico itself will make an appearance later in the book, when Cuicatl's new album fails and she takes a brief but transformative trip to Mexico City, D.F. At this point, Valdes again takes the opportunity to reiterate her views on (not) being labeled Latina in the United States, this time through the figure of Cuicatl, the (at least formerly) radicalized "mexica" chica, all brown and proud of her indigenous heritage.

During the course of *Dirty Girls on Top*, Cuicatl finds that her last album is too experimental for many of her fans, and except for her loyal Los Angeles enthusiasts, she confronts, for the first time, lackluster audiences on her promotional tour. The final insult comes when she reads an article in *USA Today* that pronounces that her "waning popularity 'is possibly evidence of a shift in mainstream sensibilities, away from the exotic and Hispanic.'" She explodes: "'Fuck you!' I shout at the paper. 'Could it be that my new music is just too fucking weird for the public? . . . Why do you have to make me your fucking spokesperson for the entire Latino world?'" (173). In support of Cuicatl, Lauren writes a column in which she opines (as does Valdes in real life) that "the mainstream media tend to assume Latino artists represent all things Latino when they do anything at all, whereas other Americans never seem to have that problem" (218). Cuicatl's love interest, Frank, suggests that, since the Minutemen are picketing her shows and demanding she go "back" to Mexico, she do just that. And—just because they can afford to, apparently—they fly to Mexico City that very day. Yet the scene greeting both

Cuicatl and the reader at the Mexico City airport deserves to be quoted at length, for the things it intimates both about Cuicatl and about US imaginaries about Mexico itself:

> Early in the afternoon, we land in the dense pink smog of Mexico City, a city that seems to stretch on forever out the window—the second-biggest city in the world. The airport is a crazy mess of people, and I try to duck their attention beneath my sunglasses and scarf. Frank stands between them and me. . . . He rents a Japanese hybrid car from a vendor near the airport and drives us expertly through the crowded, polluted, almost unfathomably huge city. . . . I follow Frank through the crowded streets, two blocks to the edge of the gigantic Plaza de la Constitución. It is a dreary-looking place of gray cement, and reminds me of all those scenes of protests in East Germany before the wall fell, except that here the gray is broken up with the bright colors of the vendors selling their food and drink and trinkets. "Where we walk, this was Aztec ground," Frank tells me. High above my head, a massive Mexican flag waves in the breeze. The air is filthy, like Los Angeles but a million times worse. He stops beneath the flag, and we look around. "This," he tells me, "is the third-largest public square in the world." (175)

Radway has shown how particular uses of language in the romance novel serve distinct readerly as well as narrative functions. She asserts the function of "marked redundancy and intertextual repetition" of a limited set of descriptors (in chica lit, for example, every hot Latino man has either a "chiseled chin" or "chiseled body"; his hands are invariably "strong," his eyes are wide and brown with "long lashes," and his gaze is "soulful"). The very fact that these descriptors occur over and over again, in not one but virtually every chica lit story I have studied, rather than boring the reader instead reassures the reader by the very familiarity of the words, and furthermore ensures that the text seems as "transparent" to the reader as possible by "obviating the need for self-conscious interpretation" (Radway 196). The world in which the romance novel—and its offspring such as chica lit—is set is always, in other words, easily knowable through these linguistic devices. Even if the content, setting, character's personalities, time, and place may be different—and therefore interesting, even exciting—

from book to book, there is no "difficult reading" to trip up the reader as she consumes the story.

The ease and "knowability" of the narrative's world and elision of the need for interpretive skills are also elements of the chica lit novel. That is, chica lit gives the reader the appearance of "realism" in that the reader is made to feel as if she knows the world in which these chica heroines live, and can therefore relate to them and their problems. Thus, the very relatability of the chica heroine, and her world, to the reader provides the energy for these books' prescriptive ends. Especially if she is steeped in the presumably transparent language, relatable characters, and a seemingly "real," knowable world of the story, the reader unconsciously accepts these novels' premises at the same time that she feels the pleasure of the familiar in the act of reading them.

If, as with Valdes's *Dirty Girls on Top*, the book includes unknown and potentially frightening spaces like Cuicatl's views of Mexico City, two techniques are employed to bring what might seem too foreign and threatening into the familiar space of the chica lit world. First, Radway points out, attention to previously unknown details are given to the reader in such a way as to appear as "information" that the reader can then add to her store of interesting facts about other places and times. In this scenario, Frank (who is Cuicatl's manager and lawyer, and as an older man who, it is clear to the reader, is madly in love with Cuicatl, is seen as trustworthy) gives her a tour not so much of Mexico City itself as of its past glories. Frank leads her through a relatively standard (in the tourist sense) running exposition on various pre-Columbian peoples who inhabited the valley of Mexico City, ending with a visit to Teotihuacán and a climb to the top of the Pyramid of the Sun (179). Thus, the reader can come away with "knowledge" about the glories of the Aztec empire without actually having to think much at all about the lives of contemporary Mexicans.

Second, the novel engages in reiterations of easily imagined, rather banal descriptive language—the city is huge, big, "second-biggest," massive, "third-largest," "almost unfathomably huge," crowded, filthy, and polluted. There are parallels to familiar scenes from the real world of the reader: it "reminds me of all those scenes of protest," it is "like Los Angeles." The familiar evocation of Mexicans as loving bright colors is included: "the bright colors of the vendors selling their food and drink and trinkets." The transparency of language and familiarity of descriptions eases the reader into this potentially estranging scene. The reader might not think much of present-day Mexico City, but she now has an easy vocabulary to think it with. Radway argues that such effortlessness of reading marked not as "work" but as "pleasure," masks "the interpretive character of the act of reading" so that the reader is prompted to accept as "fact" the world given to her.

Even more importantly, Radway suggests that through an immersion into a narrative world that requires little or no effort to apprehend, a world that can easily be pictured and thus believed, readers can also "believe in the possibility of a romantic relationship they have never experienced." I would add that readers can believe in the possibility—more, in the *desirability*—of other things they have never experienced, such as an ethnic sensibility made easy by material wealth. Frank and Cuicatl get on a plane to Mexico at a whim; Cuicatl receives celebrity baskets full of goodies, she and Frank zoom through crowded, presumably dangerous Mexico City in a rental car with no worries. This is an easeful, soothing ethnic sensibility whose access to resources and "roots" in an imagined pre-Columbian past transcend the poverty, pollution, danger, crowdedness, and general "grayness" of present-day Mexico City. As Cuicatl muses,

> I look out at the undulating crowds of people, and I get chills. Mexico. Here they are, millions upon millions of human beings, almost all of them living with much less than I have, *and we are all united.* My history lies here. . . . *I have earned enough in the past few years to live off of for the next thirty. I do not have the worries of most of the people in Mexico*, in the postcolonial world that has tried, and failed, to rob us of our past. How can you rob us of the proof of the pyramids? How can you rob us of the brown of our skin? (177, my emphasis).

Here, the seeming transparency of the language, even of the rhetorical gestures toward an ethnic sense of solidarity—allows the reader an ease of reading; there are no difficult ideas, no clever or unusual language. Everything, in other words, is laid out or gestured to in a way that, as Radway puts it, combats "ambiguity." Cuicatl does not have to worry (about anything) like the average Mexican, yet she and they are somehow brought together, through the pyramids and their "brown skin." Dirt-poor anonymous Mexicans and a wealthy, Mexican American Cuicatl become, with an ease that is breathtaking, a united "us."

In this sense, such scenes serve the ideological function of asserting both the problematic nature of "Mexico" and its inhabitants (teeming, dirty, poor, overwhelming) and assuaging readerly and/ or publishing anxiety about the knotty question of Mexican American Cuicatl's relationship to a scary, dirty, unsafe Mexico. The text reaches past any material or physical relationship with the teeming Mexican millions, to a place of "brown skin" and transcendent Aztec "heritage." In fact, it is not actually contemporary Mexico City, but the ancient city Teotihuacán that will—in fact, must—also be the place of discovery of a transcendent heterosexual love. On top of the Pyramid of the Sun, Cuicatl and Frank consummate their love: "overwhelmed with love, and happiness, and peace. . . . And as a nearly complete darkness falls over us, we remove our clothes, and just like our ancestors before us, we make love at the top of the world" (179). Here, the assertion of "feeling pre-Columbian" (Bost, *Encarnación* 42) snap-locks into place with the discovery of true love, while the familiar and seductive language of entitlement—wealth, mobility, and especially the right, as American tourists, to take off their clothes and make love in a public Mexican space—has its own sense of familiarity and pleasure. The reader's investment in the entitlement and pleasure of the main characters reassures her that nothing bad will happen to the couple while they are in this potentially scary place. Encouragingly, there are no hidden meanings here.

Rather, in the Mexico of Cuicatl and Frank, the reader plays witness to the way in which "Mexico" can function as forwarding the project of Americanization via what purports to be an authentically emotional exploration of an ancient Mexican heritage. As readers, we are of course aware that Mexico is a land of endemic poverty, but we only have to dwell on this fact for a brief and fleeting moment. Then, seductively, we feel Cuicatl's "connection" to the presumed ancient Aztec world, achieved almost instantaneously by way of her wealth and its ability to provide access to safe places in Mexico. Thus, it is her fame—re-energized by ideas about how to "maximize" her celebrity— that will finally, after the six hundred and some pages altogether of these two novels, deliver Cuicatl into a full, heterosexually coupled, materially American (-Mexican) celebrity. The added appeal of her "authentic" relationship to Mexico depends on the proper connections to her "roots" in a pre-Columbian Mexico, safely contained in its ruins and tourist discourses, thus avoiding the taint of contemporary Mexico and its problems. Even Cuicatl's truncated remarks about poverty and the hegemony of the United States, scattered throughout this second book, are folded away into a discourse of "heritage" and the rewards of celebrity motherhood. Indeed, after their trip, Frank suggests that Cuicatl should be aware "of the power you have, and we should be thinking about ways to maximize that if we can. . . . So they can't go on pretending we just got here again. . . . You know what we need to do? Get your name out. It has little to do with the music . . . so I think we should start working on raising public awareness of you now. . . . The way everyone else does it. . . . With sex and babies. You get married, or you have a baby, or you adopt a baby, or something like that" (220). Frank's suggestions on how Cuicatl should capitalize on her "Mexica-rocker" fame are consistent with the market language of commodification (in this case, making fame itself a commodity), intertwined with the romance formula at the heart of chica lit. Fictions like these reveal the ways a mass-marketed "Latina" product is unable to encompass questions of immigration, save negatively: "So they can't go on pretending we just got here again." To counter this, Cuicatl "went and found herself a couple of Chicano activists" who couldn't have a baby and becomes their surrogate (322): "Her manager, Frank . . . had the gossip press in it from the start, and all the stories talk about what a great humanitarian Cuicatl is" (323). Finally, "Having that baby made her want to have one of her own. . . . So now they're going to start trying" (323).

As an assimilated Mexican American, Cuicatl's name change from Amber and her radicalization as a "mexica" in the first book are, here, made ready for easy consumption via discourses of marketing and domesticity. The best way that "they" will be unable to "pretend we just got here again" is through Cuicatl's ascendence to both motherhood and American celebrity.

An imagined "Mexico," or better yet "Mexican culture," haunts almost all the chica lit fiction I have discussed here, as from a distance. Here, Mexico becomes, for those with enough financial capital to avoid its poverty-stricken crowds, a fantasy place that can help various of the *sucias* with access either to their "roots," or to a wellspring of creativity, or to a *domesticated* location away from the hustle and bustle of the United States. As we have seen, Cuicatl's (brief) visit to Mexico transforms her connection to her "heritage," not coincidentally turning that heritage once again into material for fame, fortune, and most priceless of all, a celebrity vision of romantic heterosexual union and domestic bliss.

At the end of *Dirty Girls on Top*, Usnavys tells us that Lauren is contemplating going to Mexico to write a book. Although Lauren is half Cuban, her plans continue the long tradition in the United States of imagining Mexico as a kind of artists' colony, where creative juices can be replenished by a more primitive pace of life. (In the third book, *Lauren's Saints of Dirty Faith*, Lauren never makes it to Mexico, although she does end up in *New* Mexico.) As Usnavys sums it up, Elizabeth also "dropped a big old bomb on us the first night we were here, *m'ija*, and said they've been talking about buying a house in Baja, Mexico" (where by 2007 several hundred thousand American expatriates actually lived, especially along the coast [Nevaer]). Finally, Elizabeth's partner Margo's money gives Elizabeth the freedom to "decide to . . . stay home with Gordon [her adopted African child] full time" (324). Indeed, through the domestication of their romantic relationships (having babies and stable families—thus normalizing Elizabeth's homosexuality along the way), as well as through their financial freedom, both Cuicatl's and Elizabeth's arrival at a happy ending paradoxically enough renders the *use* of Mexico as a kind of annex to the dream of a well-off American family life.

In these novels, "Mexico" is an abstraction upon which can be projected the fears and desires of the American Latina. Neither Marcela of *How to Become Latina* nor Alexis of *Playing with Boys* feel anything when confronted with displays of Mexicannness, unless as with Alexis they are explicitly connected to American patriotism.[1] This imagined Mexico also functions simultaneously as a no-strings-attached "land of mañana" enjoyment and specter of an almost-failed state, overwhelmed by the poor and the desperate looking to flee.

Thus, for chica lit, Mexico is constructed, in the beginnings of the twenty-first century, as a deeply ambiguous—and often imaginary—set of contradictory signs. For Mexican American chica heroines, especially like Kathy Cano-Murillo's Star in *Waking Up in the Land of Glitter* but also, to a lesser extent, Marta Acosta's Milagro in the *Casa Dracula* series, these include Mexico as a "heritage" site from which to capitalize on personal style and design. For Tamara, the chica heroine of Mary Castillo's *Hot Tamara*, Mexico represents the working-class kitsch of Spanish-speaking parents and, even more telling, the contempt of Mexican Americans (like her Nana Rosa) for those on the other side of the border. It is Nana Rosa who nixes teaching Spanish to the kids: "*You don't want them to be like those Mexicans who don't realize they're in America*" (5). Such an admonition could well be the perfect catchphrase for every chica lit heroine in the fictions examined here, summing up, as every good behavior manual does, what one must learn about proper American behavior.

How to Become Cuban American

> I ask where he's from. "America," he says with a mixture of pride and complicity, as do all Yankees who sneak into Cuba. "It's *norte-americano*," I say, playfully scolding. "We Cubans are offended that you claim the whole continent for yourselves." He's not listening.
> —LISA WIXON, *DIRTY BLONDE AND HALF CUBAN*

Like Mexico, US popular imaginings about Cuba are ambivalent at best, complicated with a willful ignorance about both nations. Both nations occupy a place in the US mental map as a "Here Be Dragons" space, onto which can be projected scenarios both frightening and alluring. The fifty-year-old US embargo against a country that lies only ninety miles off the US coast leaves a large arena for such imaginings. In this final chapter, I explore a fiction where Cuba plays simultaneously the space of the foreign unknown and the country of the American romantic imagination.

Born and raised in a diplomatic family with white privilege and material wealth, like Marcela in *How to Become Latina*, the main character of Lisa Wixon's *Dirty Blonde and Half Cuban*, Alysia, uncovers a family secret—in this case, that her biological father is Cuban—and sets off to Cuba (illegally) to find him. Her savings stolen, she finally finds she must *resolver*, or make do, like other Cubans who have straight jobs or professions that don't give them enough money, by being a *jinetera*: having sex with tourists for money and presents. Alysia's identity crisis, where she muses that "Some days I'm more heavily Cuban. On others, I weigh in more American" (4), is here the motivating factor for her "job." Indeed, the choice of seeing Cuba through the optics of *jineterismo* brings the reader back, strangely enough, to a world with which the chica lit reader would be familiar. This is a world where the main character, despite many obstacles, gets her (fabulous Caribbean) man; lots of sex, although much of it is awkward; and a truly fantastic (at least for Cubans) level of access to luxury goods; and finally finds her Cuban father. Many of the narrative themes here also echo those found in chica lit: a heroine with a good education and middle-class values, who nevertheless must overcome a series of seemingly insuperable obstacles.

Like many chica lit books, Wixon's begins in medias res: "I felt his hand on my bare shoulder, and it was all over" (4). Alysia is sitting at a restaurant in Havana, working on her notebooks, when a foreign tourist buys her a drink and propositions her. We know that she's "more heavily Cuban" at that moment, as he does not recognize a fellow American citizen; and to cement this misrecognition, he assumes she is a *jinetera*, the Cuban slang for a "jockey" who "rides" wealthy foreigners for money and presents. As she gathers up her money afterwards, she is "at that moment . . . only Cuban" (5). This sentiment is confirmed when Alysia confesses the transaction to her Cuban friend Camila who responds, "You're a Cuban girl now" (6). Yet Camila's own combination of brilliance (she's a heart surgeon, no less) and beauty bring her access to luxuries via her many foreign "boyfriends," an access that represents, according to Wixon herself, levels of material wealth most Cubans could never dream of. The *jineteras* that Alysia hangs out with wear Armani, Miu Miu, and Marc Jacobs clothes, Jean-Paul Gaultier perfume, Chanel lipstick, and Christian Dior shoes.

Despite Alysia's apparent lack of physical grace, her terrible salsa dancing, and the endlessly bad sex she has with various tourists, Cuba, as every good romance/chica lit reader knows, is where she will meet the man of her dreams. At a club filled with "faces and bodies culled from the best of human genetics," she meets her great Cuban love, Rafael: he's "tall and broad, with a square jaw and a tousle of clove-colored hair and eyes. His smooth, *dulce de leche* skin stretches over naturally curved, abundant muscles" (60). Although she resists him, Rafael will win her heart; since he too is a *jinetero* he won't judge her for being the same. Like all romantic endings, the heroine willingly sacrifices in order to be with love and family. Literally on the road to the airport, Alysia realizes where her priorities lie—with love and family—and her father turns the car around, so that she can live in Cuba with Rafael and her family, still working as a *jinetera*. Because her choice of how to make a living is counterintuitive to a chica lit "happy ending," *Dirty Blonde* couches Alysia's decision to stay in a place without toilet paper in the language of a kind of Cuban American ethnic "destiny." "Each day," muses Alysia after her decision to stay, "I grow more convinced this was the destiny my mother turned her back on; a destiny that was hers, perhaps, and certainly, unequivocally, mine" (245).

In Wixon's book, then, Cuba is both land of delicious bodies and great sex, unromantic underwear, and no toilet paper. Even though *Dirty Girls*'s Mexico and *Dirty Blonde*'s Cuba are distinctly different in tone, structure, and function, at the same time Wixon must work hard to extract the differences involved in being a woman in revolutionary Cuba from the potentially deadly samenesses of romance and chick lit conventions, conflicts, and happy endings. Yet Wixon's choice of profession for Alysia is made legible through the context of a country where the pull of hard currency—dollars or Euros—exerts a centrifugal force on the Cuban economy as well as on the desires of Cubans themselves. Although Alysia elects to stay in Cuba, the uneasy clash of her (unusual) privilege as a *jinetera* with the straitened circumstances of Cuba itself seems to highlight, in an aversive way, Cuba's "difference" from the United States.

After Wixon's book, published in 2006, became a hit, she published a brief article, "Cuba for Dummies," in the *Washington Post*. In it, she lambasts several of what she identifies as the most enduring myths as well as political falsehoods about Cuba perpetuated in the United States:

> I lived in Havana for nearly a year without permission from the
> United States. I talked to Cubans and found out what they had to

say. Nothing bad happened to me. . . . [Cuban] society would not be so closed if the current administration hadn't tightened restrictions that ban Americans from visiting Cuba and meeting locals. More egregious is the U.S. economic embargo, which has served only to empower Castro while impoverishing Cubans. . . . [M]ost important, Cubans adore their country. Why would they leave? What they want is to stay home *and* have economic and political reforms. They know the United States can be scary for immigrants. Our poor are much worse off than theirs.

Finally, she ends with a finger shaking at all those who think they can benefit from a breakdown of Cuban society: "Fidel and his ragtag forces were capable of taking Cuba in 1959 because its people were fed up with the system under U.S. proxy Fulgencio Batista. The whole mess will happen all over again if the Cubans are not left alone to determine their own political and social fate. . . . Unless you're part of the family, stay out of it." Just as Valdes's authorial voice, expressed through her narrators such as Lauren and Usnavys, is clearly meant to convey information to the reader, Wixon's main character Alysia serves as the eyes and voice for information about the people who live in Cuba now. The choice of this novel's setting, in revolutionary "Special Period" Cuba, and the apparently nonjudgmental choice of a career of *jineterismo* for Alysia, mark the text with an oppositional sensibility that seems to be the reverse of the sensibility found in descriptions of the "Mexico" Cuicatl briefly visits.

Is it possible to coherently think through questions of ethnic identity and difference—Mexican American, Cuban American— outside the constraining borders of the United States? bell hooks maintains that "Difference can seduce precisely because the mainstream imposition of sameness is a provocation that terrorizes," in the sense of making identity "fixed, static, a condition of containment and death" (*Black Looks* 22–23). In this sense, the commodification, and subsequent ease of consumption, of Otherness that a corporate, or commodified, vision of multiculturalism seems to offer—for instance, in the proliferation of ethnic and racialized niche markets in the publishing of women's popular literature—can relieve the terror of sameness. At the same time the way in which multicultural experience is structured as commodity ensures that, as hooks puts it, "the encounter with the Other does not require that one relinquish . . . one's main-stream positionality," that is, one's privilege (23). Readers of chica lit who are not Latina, for example, can "sample" a bit of difference, yet can walk away unchanged.

For chica lit authors, their characters, and their readers, however, it is *precisely* the "mainstream positionality" of a cultural American citizenship to which these fictions aim to provide a roadmap. In this sense, it is even more important to remember that the "mainstream imposition of sameness" represents a seductive place of gender, race, and class privilege. For those who are the targets of pejorative imag-inings, to be invited into the house of sameness, of privilege, can seem to be infinitely desirable. The payment required is the Other's willing-ness to be fundamentally changed.

Notes

1. In this book I use the general label "Latina/o" to designate those large groups who originated from a Hispanophone Latin/South American or Caribbean nation, such as Nuyoricans, Cuban Americans, Dominican Americans, etc. For what I would normally call Chicano/a characters, however, I use "Mexican American." All except one of the chica lit novels I examine here either uses the term "Chicana/o" pejoratively, or uses instead "Mexican American" or even sometimes "Mexican" (confusingly, for characters born in the United States). Thus, I use only the more activist term "Chicano/a" when discussing the ethnic politics of these novels.

2. In chica lit, the term "American" is reserved exclusively for, and stops at the boundaries of, the United States. Hence, I will sometimes put quotation marks around this term to highlight "America's" exclusion of the rest of the continent. Here, I consistently feel the lack of a single term in English for "United States citizen," such as Spanish has: "estadounidense."

Introduction: A Regular American Life

1. See, for example, Erin Hurt's, Amanda Morrison's, and Catherine Ramírez's analyses of Valdes's *Dirty Girls Social Club* books as well as the work of Elena Sáez-Machado, Arlene Dávila, Frances Negrón-Muntaner, Renato Rosaldo, Frances Aparicio, Juan Flores, and more on representations of race, gender, and ethnicity within the (neoliberal) marketplace.

2. For instance, the Latina consumer is often presented as culturally (use of this word often implies an innate, even biological connection: "it's in the blood") passionate yet family-oriented. Yet she is also just the same as you or me, doing everyday things like going to work and working out at the gym; on the other hand, she seems to consume Latino music and dancing to an unprecedented degree. These are, indeed, a few of the notions one can glean from the trade magazine *Ad Age*, which just released its 2014 "Hispanic Fact

Pack." Along with numbers showing the largest Hispanic ad agencies, radio, television, and cable companies, what technologies Latinos use the most, and so on, are advertisements to advertisers—meta-ads, one might say—whose pitches make vague references to the love Hispanics have for their culture. Batanga Media, for example, avers that "Latin music / is not one genre / a channel / a trend / Latin music is culture"; they urge advertisers to hook up to their audience through Batanga's Latin music streaming app, "with millions of listeners connecting to their culture every day" ("Hispanic Fact Pack").

3. I prefer the idea of "niche" women's fiction to the term "subgenre," particularly since I am emphasizing both the blurring of generic borders and the marketing world's ongoing quest to create and fill demographic niches.

4. Nevertheless, publishers make sure that bookstores file chica lit in its proper niche through the many references on these books' front and back covers to other identifiably Latina authors of chica lit as well as these covers' design references to chick lit books, slightly skewed toward the "hot and spicy" end of the spectrum.

5. The British economist John Williams became linked to such practices when in 1989 he coined the term "the Washington Consensus" in his paper "What Washington Means by Policy Reform." There, he referred to "10 policy instruments about whose proper deployment Washington can muster a reasonable degree of consensus." "Washington" here included "both the political Washington of Congress and senior members of the administration and the technocratic Washington of the international financial institutions, the economic agencies of the US government, the Federal Reserve Board, and the think tanks" as well as the Institute for International Economics (np). This consensus came together over a period of the ten years, between 1982 and the beginning of the 1990s, of an alarming Latin American debt crisis, when the above-named entities demanded deep economic adjustments in exchange for loaning Latin American countries money. Williams makes it clear that the ten topics his paper addresses are "*policy instruments* rather than objectives or outcomes" and is critical of the lip service "Washington" has paid to "the promotion of democracy and human rights, suppression of the drug trade, preservation of the environment, and control of population growth." Despite a nuanced approach, however, this paper ensured that his ideas are forever associated, for critics as well as admirers of neoliberalism, with a broader orientation toward a strongly free-market-based, anti–social welfare, pro-privatization economy.

6. Neoliberal ideas particularly about the place of social responsibility (private rather than supported by government aid) began, in fact, to be adopted in response to the turn toward conservatism orchestrated by the Reagan administration's demonization of the previous Carter government, itself plagued by a severe recession and the Iraq hostage crisis.

7. As a quick glance at the small number of Latinas/os who actually attain the middle class shows, many of our chica heroines' achievements often hinge on certain privileges not usually extended, in the United States, to Latinas/os as a group. Such privileges often include the possession of, at least, a cultural whiteness: a middle-class income and/or profession, a light complexion (yes, there are light-skinned, even blonde, blue-eyed Latinas/Chicanos), dropping the Spanish accent marks from first and last names, and loosening ties in general to Spanish as well as to one's family's country of origin. Attaining material success may also depend on having access to generational economic and cultural capital, which many Latinos and Mexican Americans do not regularly have.

8. Teaching chica lit as well as other women's genre fiction, I have often heard my students express their wonderment that, the first time they read these popular books, they didn't notice any of the strategies, contradictions, or problems with the narrative that they now, in close critical readings, clearly see. This might seem obvious, given the ephemeral nature of such fictions that are meant to be consumed quickly, but it bears repeating nevertheless; such "entertainment" is so entertaining, so to speak, because ideologically speaking its narrative strategies and the reader's familiarity with plot conventions tend to encourage quick reading and suppress critical thinking, which is widely assumed to be the opposite of pleasurable reading.

9. As Erin Hurt maintains in her incisive reading of *Dirty Girls Social Club*, "the chick lit genre . . . severely constrains [chica lit's] cultural work. . . . The contradiction of the content's complex work of exploring and redefining identity and the genre's need to produce and sell the literary equivalent of cotton candy produces an ambivalent Latinidad that argues for a common American sameness, but also insists on a distinct ethnicity" (134).

10. As I have noted in "Are You a *Pura Latina*?," ethnic women's magazines like *Latina* "offer points of accommodation with, as well as points of resistance to," a mass media still engaged in privileging whiteness and middle-class access to resources. *Latina* regularly offers its readers "examples of Latina [and less so, Chicana] success stories . . . [and] Latina-oriented advice

to women on child care, money matters, as well as on fashion and men—those *papis chulos* ('Our Finest Men') figured in each *Latina* issue" (Hedrick 149). I have also remarked on this magazine's blend of resistant narratives (sometimes contained in its sections "La Lucha/The Struggle" and "Triunfos/Successes") with what Dominick LaCapra has called the assimilative and assimilating capacity of mass culture, where "a mild and readily contained level of social and cultural criticism is the price of access to the mass media" (LaCapra 136).

11. Both in *Madame Bovary* and in *A Sentimental Education*, Gustave Flaubert savagely parodied and critiqued what he thought were the instruments of intellectual weakness and passivity for both men and women of his time: romantic and sentimental novels. In these were to be found the *idées reçues* Flaubert saw as clichéd, automatic thoughts and platitudes, and that he gathered together in a spoof dictionary of modern French stupidities.

12. Kathryn Sloane documents the place of advice manuals in the lives of upper-class women in nineteenth-century Mexico: "chapbooks provided advice for lovers, including the formula for writing love letters. Advice for courting men and women also figured prominently and included warnings that physical beauty and wealth were less important than honesty and good work habits" (90). For discussions of how young privileged Mexican women in the twentieth century were being shaped by public discourse including advice manuals, see *Sex in Revolution: Gender, Politics, and Power in Modern Mexico*, edited by Jocelyn Olcott, Mary Kay Vaughan, and Gabriela Cano.

13. Historian Sarah Leavitt examines the place of the advice manual in women's lives in the United States from the 1830s to the first part of the twenty-first century. As she informs us, "The close connection with novels gave the domestic-advice manual a familiar literary form. This format probably helped women readers to understand the emerging genre and to know what to expect. . . . Some authors [of advice manuals] even used fictional characters" (12).

14. As Leavitt notes, the New Mexican domestic advisor Fabiola Cabeza de Baca Gilbert attempted in her work to influence "both the way that Hispanic New Mexicans viewed mainstream American culture and the way that Americans all over the country viewed New Mexico" (87).

15. UrbanLatino.com's "About Us" page has this to say: "As the first lifestyle and cultural publication geared to bicultural Latinos, *Urban Latino* has earned its rightful place: we are the premier magazine for both male and female Latinos in the United States. Since 1994, we have been exploring the

contemporary lives of a new generation that is embarking on its own distinct journey. Poised to be the largest market in the new millennium, Latinos will forge ahead, delineating our path, setting our own goals, creating our own agenda, and interpreting and living out distinct and intertwined lives. We are on the cusp of a new culture forged from the vastness of Latin American heritage and the richness of contemporary U.S. society" (np).

16. As Warren French has noted, it was Robert Fair de Graffe, himself long in the reprint book industry, who started Pocket Books in 1939 and, following earlier but less ambitious publishers such as Mercury Press and Modern Age Books, reprinted already popular books in paperback form (256–57). De Graffe made paperbacks in a "pocket" size, and sold them in grocery and drug stores as well as in department stores and bookstands. By the 1970s, the mall bookstores Walden Books and B. Dalton had redesigned the bookstore along the lines of the grocery store, organized to display, choose, and sell, quickly and efficiently, "recognizable products that sold on impulse"—which often meant genre fiction, especially for women (Epstein 105). At least until the failures of these companies in the Great Recession and the advent of electronic reading platforms like the Kindle, there had also come to be the comfort bookstores—such as Barnes & Noble or Borders. Such bookstores made the consumption of books even more appealing, as (especially women) customers could not only browse but also sit and read in nooks and cafés with a reasonable amount of privacy.

17. American scholars of popular women's writing in the twentieth and twenty-first centuries include Pam Regis, who in her *A Natural History of the Romance Novel* also shows the links as well as differences between nineteenth- and late twentieth-century women's writing.

18. Arlene Dávila and Agustín Láo-Montes's edited collection, *Mambo Montage: The Latinization of New York*, introduces the term "Latinization" as multiple discourses of *latinidad*. They note, "It is not only possible to distinguish between governmental, corporate, and academic discourses. . . . but also [possible] to analyze how latinidad is produced through the work of the Latino community . . . this overall production of discourses of latinidad is what we call Latinization" (4).

19. As Ramírez has written, "These tropicalizing signs render their Latinaness intelligible to the reader. They also define latinidad not in terms of a single language or common history, social space, or political vision, but as a lifestyle and product." Quoting Frances Aparicio and Susana Chávez-Silverman, she goes on, "When reduced to 'reformulations of cultural icons,' such as

'food and clothing, language, and popular music,' latinidad is more easily commodified and consumed" (14). See discussions of Latinization in *Mambo Montage: The Latinization of New York City*, *Tropicalizations: Transcultural Representations of Latinidad*, and *The Diaspora Strikes Back: Caribeño Tales of Learning and Turning*, just to mention a few.

Chapter 1: Genre and the Romance Industry

1. The Chicano literary critic Ramón Saldívar has argued that "in the twenty-first century, the relationship between race and social justice, race and identity, and indeed, race and history requires the new generation of writers to invent a new 'imaginary' for thinking about the nature of a just society" (1). Here, Saldívar has begun to think through the "postracial" or "postethnic" narratives of twenty-first-century Latina/o narratives: "Of greater moment today is the redeployment of arguments and strategies for understanding anew the way that 'race' is constructed by the power of white supremacy and deconstructed by the lived experience of contemporary people of color. The narrative of this redefinition posits race and racialization as a *doing*, a communal ongoing system of processes" (2).

Frederick Aldama's critical approach also addresses a "post" in ethnic criticism without assuming that we are now past white supremacist capitalist patriarchy. Aldama uses magical realism as a theoretical framework to examine a variety of ethnic and postcolonial texts that he finds escape the very moments that shaped them. For example, Aldama disputes the assumed realism of writings such as Oscar Zeta Acosta's *Autobiography of a Brown Buffalo* (1974). Instead, he argues that even at the moment Acosta was writing, he and others were reworking their narratives away from what were fast becoming pseudo-sociological expectations about what constituted "realistic" ethnic writing (64). Both Aldama and Saldívar see ethnic and racialized narratives "as a *doing*." That is, postethnic narratives actively participate in a constant process of (re)imagining and negotiating ethnic lives, rather than as essentialist or static folklore or ethnographic accounts of racialized realities.

2. In their analysis of the structure of handbooks for writing romances, Dirk de Geest and An Goris note that turn-of-the-twenty-first-century romance fiction advertises itself as fit for the new young woman, who would not be interested in the "bodice-ripper," "old-fashioned" romances of the popular imagination. As they note, "handbooks present themselves as being up-to-date ('gone are the days,' 'these days'); they articulate the norms and con-

straints of today's romance genre. The heroine is no longer waiting passively and patiently for a hero who will rescue her from her lethargic existence and introduce her to real life and passion. On the contrary, she leads an active and independent life, professionally as well as in her personal capacity; she freely takes the initiative and seems quite happy to remain single (but this, needless to say, does not prevent her from falling in love with the future hero)" (99).

3. They have yet to materialize, although earlier this year Valdes threw out an idea to her Facebook audience: "For the new dgsc [Dirty Girls Social Club] Usnavys book, I'm thinking of sending Usnavys to a foreign country for a visiting marketing professorship and having her undergo a major spiritual awakening after befriending a mysterious woman who turns out to have been an angel. What country should she go to?"

4. Citing differences with her publisher, however, Valdes self-published the third installment of the *Dirty Girls* trio, *Lauren's Saints of Dirty Faith*, both in hard copy and in e-book format.

5. Valdes and other chica lit authors have self-published entire books, novellas, and single chapters on Kindle, such as an erotic chapter Valdes felt was too steamy to include in *Lauren's Saints of Dirty Faith*. It describes in graphic detail her *Dirty Girls* character Lauren's sexual encounter with the now-infamous outrageously sexy cowboy, a thinly veiled character reference to her own romance with "the cowboy" in her autobiographical *The Cowboy and the Feminist: An Unlikely Love Story*, published by Penguin Press in 2013. She insisted that the cowboy, with his traditional views about sex roles, had finally allowed her to give up her own "radical second-wave feminism" in learning "to submit, to trust, to become one with a man." Asserting that "relationships are in crisis," Valdes maintained in this interview that "If we want functional, healthy relationships, we cannot deny our biology anymore. We have to let men be men, and let women be women. Simple as that" ("A conversation"). This book, and her many assertions of the benefits of "submitting" to a man such as the Cowboy, are now infamous for Valdes's online repudiation—almost as soon as the book came out—of the Cowboy and her subsequent description of their relationship as abusive.

6. Latinos of course are not uniformly brown but range across the spectrum of racialized "color"; and whiteness itself can be racialized. For example, most folks do not think of white-skinned, blonde Cameron Diaz as Latina although her father is Cuban, while the clear class and cultural affiliations and accented English mark light-skinned, dark-haired comedian and actor John Leguizamo as not white.

Chapter 2: Class and Taste

1. See discussions of the connections between style, shopping, consumerism, and taste in, for example, Stephanie Harzewski's *Chick Lit and Postfeminism* and Suzanne Ferriss and Mallory Young's *Chick Lit: The New Woman's Fiction*, as well as essays such as Deborah Philips's "Shopping for Men"; these are just a few of the many critical works that examine the ways these intertwine with one another.

2. The reader with knowledge of the history of Latino/a politics will immediately recognize MEChA, or Movimiento Estudantil Chicano de Aztlán, as a politicized student movement that traces its foundation to the Chicano manifesto *El Plan de Santa Bárbara* in 1969 ("About Us"). The latter reference to the Latino Student's Business Association, then, evokes conservative, assimilationist organizations and special-interest magazines such as the long-standing League of Latin American Citizens (LULAC), organized in 1930 by middle-class Mexican Americans, or *HispanicBusiness*, a magazine begun in 1979.

3. In her study of twenty-first-century middle-class Mexican Americans, Jody Vallejo finds that as recent sociological research has indicated, "Women bear an additional ethnic stereotypical burden as Latina professionals and entrepreneurs must also contend with gendered stereotypes that whites hold of Latinas. They might be middle class, but [non-Latino whites assume] . . . that Latinas live within a patriarchal ethnic community where early childbearing, motherhood, and a 'cultural' desire for large families are valued over education or professional success" (162–63).

4. Acosta explains, "'Assimilated' means that [Milagro] speaks English fluently and is part of American culture and society. She's conscious of the difference between US-born and raised Latinos and immigrant Latinos. The media often uses 'Latino/Hispanic' as synonymous with 'immigrant'—out of sloppiness or ignorance or both, I don't know. Are my experiences and perspectives different from my mother, who was born in Mexico and spent her youth there? Absolutely. Are they different than a high-school friend who was raised in a privileged family in Lima? Yes. For Milagro, being assimilated means that she completely owns her identity as an American, too. She never lets anyone deny her . . . that" (np).

Chapter 3: Latinization and Authenticity

1. As the *National Journal*, an online news magazine, reported in October 17, 2013, the "salsa is overtaking ketchup" story actually "broke" in 1992. Alex Seitz-Wald reports that "this is just the latest in long line of stories using culinary sales as a marker of demographic change. . . . David Weiss, the president of New York–based Packaged Facts Inc., the same market-research firm that the AP quotes in its 2013 story, told the [*New York*] *Times* back then that 'the taste for salsa is as mainstream as apple pie these days'" ("Salsa Overtook Ketchup Twenty Years Ago," http://www.nationaljournal.com/politics/salsa -overtook-ketchup-20-years-ago-20131017).

2. This is evidently a misspelling and regendering of "el cucuy," a Mexican word for the "boogey man."

3. Although the book calls it "wedding soup," this is clearly Mexican *mole poblano*, a spicy, unsweetened chocolate sauce thickened with tortillas and pine nuts and served over turkey for special occasions.

Chapter 4: Conclusion

1. Again, the problem of authorial intent arises here—that Alexis clearly sees herself as a card-carrying member of the Republican Party makes her ideas and comments, given Valdes's own very public liberal politics at the time, probably satirical; yet as I have noted, it's difficult to tell who the target is, given Valdes's equal-opportunity snarkiness.

Works Cited

"About Us." *Movimiento Estudiantil Chican@ de Aztlán Official National Website*. Movimiento Estudiantil Chican@ de Aztlán, n.d. Web. 8 Apr. 2009.

Acosta, Marta. *Bride of Casa Dracula*. New York: Pocket Books, 2008.

———. *Happy Hour at Casa Dracula*. New York: Pocket Books, 2006.

———. *Haunted Honeymoon*. New York: Gallery Books, 2010.

———. *Midnight Brunch*. New York: Pocket Books, 2007.

Aldama, Frederick. *Postethnic Narrative Criticism: Magicorealism in Oscar "Zeta" Acosta, Ana Castillo, Julie Dash, Hanif Kureishi, and Salman Rushdie*. Austin: University of Texas Press, 2003.

———. *Routledge Concise History of Latino/a Literature*. New York: Routledge, 2013.

Álvarez, Maribel. *Made in Mexico: Souvenirs, Artisans, Shoppers and the Meanings of Other "Border-Type Things."* Diss. University of Arizona, 2003.

Aparicio, Frances. "On Multiculturalism and Privilege: A Latina Perspective." *American Quarterly* 46.4 (1994): 575–88.

Aparicio, Frances, and Susana Chávez-Silverman, eds. *Tropicalizations: Transcultural Representations of Latinidad*. Hanover, NH: Dartmouth College, University Press of New England, 1997.

Armstrong, Nancy. *Desire and Domestic Fiction: A Political History of the Novel*. New York: Oxford University Press, 1987.

———. "Some Call it Fiction: On the Politics of Domesticity." *Literary Theory: An Anthology*. 2nd ed. Ed. Julie Rivkin and Michael Ryan. Malden, MA: Blackwell, 2004. 567–83.

Baym, Nina. *Woman's Fiction: A Guide to Novels by and about Women in America, 1820–70*. 2nd ed. Ithaca, NY: Cornell University Press, 1993.

"Book Parties Generate Publicity." *Party Launch*. Party Launch, n.d. Web. 8 Apr. 2009.

Bost, Suzanne. *Encarnación: Illness and Body Politics in Chicana Feminist Literature*. New York: Fordham University Press, 2010.

———. "Women and Chile at the Alamo: Feeding U.S. Colonial Mythology." *Nepantla: Views from the South* 4.3 (2003): 493–522.

Bourdieu, Pierre. *Distinction: A Social Critique of the Judgement of Taste*. 1984. New York: Routledge, 2010.

Bruce-Novoa, Juan. *RetroSpace: Collected Essays on Chicano Literature, Theory, and History*. Houston: Arte Público Press, 1990.

Butler, Pamela, and Jigna Desai. "Manolos, Marriage, and Mantras: Chick-Lit Criticism and Transnational Feminism." *Meridians: Feminism, Race, Transnationalism* 8.2 (2008): 1–31.

Calvani, Myra. "Future of Latino Book Market Promising." *Examiner.com*. Anschutz Corporation. 25 Aug. 2012. Web. 28 Dec. 2013.

Caminero-Santangelo, Marta. "Latinidad." *The Routledge Companion to Latino/a Literature*. Ed. Suzanne Bost and Frances R. Aparicio. New York: Routledge, 2013. 13–24.

Cano-Murillo, Kathy. *La Casa Loca: Latino Style Comes Home: 45 Funky Craft Projects for Decorating and Entertaining*. Gloucester: Rockport Publishers, 2003.

——. *Waking Up in the Land of Glitter*. New York: Grand Central Publishing. 2010.

Carmon, Irin. "Romance Novels Are Steaming Up E-Reader Screens." *FastCompany.com*. Fast Company & Inc. 22 June 2011. Web.

"Cartas de José Martí." *La página de José Martí*. Hilda Luisa Díaz-Perera, n.d. Web.

Castillo, Debra. "Impossible Indian." *Chasqui* 35.2 (2006): 42–57.

Castillo, Mary. *Hot Tamara*. New York: Avon Trade, 2005.

——. *In Between Men*. New York: HarperCollins, 2006.

——. "My Favorite Mistake." *Friday Night Chicas: Sexy Stories from La Noche*. Mary Castillo, Berta Platas, Caridad Piñeiro, and Sofia Quintero. New York: St. Martin's Griffin, 2005.

——. *Switchcraft*. New York: HarperCollins, 2007.

Cisneros, Sandra. *The House on Mango Street*. 1984. New York: Vintage, 1991.

"*Cosmopolitan* Red Hot Reads." *Harlequin*. Harlequin Enterprises, n.d. Web.

Dalleo, Raphael, and Elena Sáez. *Latina/o Canon and the Emergence of Post-Sixties Literature*. New York: Palgrave MacMillan, 2007.

Dávila, Arlene M. *Barrio Dreams: Puerto Ricans, Latinos, and the Neoliberal City*. Berkeley: University of California Press, 2004.

——. *Latino Spin: Public Image and the Whitewashing of Race*. New York: New York University Press, 2008.

——. *Latinos, Inc: The Marketing and Making of a People*. Berkeley: University of California Press, 2001.

de Certeau, Michel. *The Practice of Everyday Life*. Trans. Steven F. Rendall. Reprint. Berkeley: University of California Press, 2011.

de Geest, Dirk, and An Goris. "Constrained Writing, Creative Writing: The Case of Handbooks for Writing Romances." *Poetics Today* 31.1 (2010): 81–106.

DiVisconte, Jessica. "The Recession and Its Effect on the Romance Genre." MS thesis. Pace University, 2009.

Epstein, Jason. *Book Business: Publishing Past, Present, and Future*. New York: W. W. Norton, 2001.

Eysturoy, Annie. *Daughters of Self-Creation: The Contemporary Chicana Novel*. Albuquerque: University of New Mexico Press, 1996.

Flores, Juan. *The Diaspora Strikes Back: Caribeño Tales of Learning and Turning*. New York: Routledge, 2009.

French, Warren. "The First Year of the Paperback Revolution." *College English* 25.4 (1964): 255–60.

Giddens, Anthony. *Modernity and Self-Identity: Self and Society in the Late Modern Age*. Cambridge, UK: Polity Press, 1991.

Gledhill, Christine. "Genre." *The Cinema Book*. Ed. Pam Cook. London: British Film Institute, 1985.

Guenther, Leah. "*Bridget Jones's Diary*: Confessing Feminism." *Modern Confessional Writing: New Critical Essays*. Ed. Jo Gill. New York: Routledge, 2006. 84–99.

Gurza, Agustín. "1999 Was the Year of the Latin Explosion." *Los Angeles Times*. 15 Aug. 2004. Web.

Harner, John. "Muebles Rústicos in Mexico and the United States." *Geographical Review* 92.3 (2002): 354–71.

Harvey, David. *The Condition of Postmodernity: An Enquiry into the Origins of Cultural Change*. New York: Wiley-Blackwell, 1991.

Harzewski, Stephanie. *Chick Lit and Postfeminism*. Charlottesville: University of Virginia, 2011.

———. "Tradition and Displacement in the New Novel of Manners." *Chick Lit: The New Woman's Fiction*. Ed. Suzanne Ferriss and Mallory Young. New York: Routledge, 2006.

Hedrick, Tace. "Are You a *Pura Latina*? or, Menudo Every Day: *Tacones* and Symbolic Ethnicity." *Footnotes: On Shoes*. Ed. Shari Benstock and Suzanne Ferris. New Brunswick: Rutgers University Press, 2001. 135–55.

"Hispanic Fact Pack: Annual Guide to Hispanic Marketing and Media." *Advertising Age*. Crain Communications. 22 July 2013. Web. 11 Oct. 2014.

hooks, bell. "Altars of Sacrifice: Re-Membering Basquiat." *Race-ing Art History: Critical Readings in Race and Art History*. Ed. Kymberly N. Pinder. New York: Routledge, 2002. 341–50.

———. "Eating the Other: Desire and Resistance." *Black Looks: Race and Representation*. Boston: South End Press, 1992. 21–39.

Horkheimer, Max, and Theodor Adorno. *The Dialectic of Enlightenment: Philosophical Fragments*. Ed. Gunzelin Schmid Noerr. Trans. Edmund Jephcott. Stanford, CA: University of Stanford Press, 2002.

"How to Write the Perfect Romance!" *Harlequin*. Harlequin Enterprises, n.d. Web.

Hurt, Erin. "Trading Cultural Baggage for Gucci Luggage: The Ambivalent *Latinidad* of Alisa Valdes-Rodriguez's *The Dirty Girls Social Club*." *MELUS: Multi-Ethnic Literature of the US* 34.3 (2009): 133–53.

Japtok, Martin. *Growing Up Ethnic: Nationalism and the Bildungsroman in African American and Jewish American Fiction*. Iowa City: University of Iowa Press, 2005.

Jones, Amelia. *Seeing Differently: A History and Theory of Identification and the Visual Arts*. New York: Routledge, 2013.

"Julia Amante." *TheLatinoAuthor.com*. n.d. Web.

LaCapra, Dominick. *Soundings in Critical Theory*. Ithaca, NY: Cornell University Press, 1989.

Landres, Marcela. "Business Plan for Writers." *Latinidad*. 2 Sep. 2006. Web.

———. "Q&A: Mary Castillo." *Latinidad*. 2 Sep. 2006. Web.

Láo-Montes, Agustín, and Arlene Dávila, eds. *Mambo Montage: The Latinization of New York*. New York: Columbia University Press, 2001.

Leavitt, Sarah. *From Catharine Beecher to Martha Stewart: A Cultural History of Domestic Advice*. Chapel Hill: University of North Carolina, 2002.

Lengel, Kerry. "Hot Chica Lit Takes a Sassy Style to Look at Latina Life." *Hispanic Trending: Documenting Latino's Imprint in America*. 18 May 2006. Web. 28 Dec. 2012.

Lewis, Oscar. "The Culture of Poverty." *Scientific American* 215.4 (1966): 19–25.

———. *Five Families: Mexican Case Studies in the Culture of Poverty*. New York: Basic Books, 1959.

———. *La Vida: A Puerto Rican Family in the Culture of Poverty—San Juan and New York*. London: Secker and Harville, 1966.

"Marcela Landres Answers Latino Writers" *La Bloga*. n.d. Web. 7 Jan. 2012.

McCracken, Ellen. "From Chapbooks to *Chica Lit*: U.S. Latina Writers and the New Literary Identity." *International Perspectives on Chicana/o Studies: "This*

World Is My Place." Ed. Catherine Leen and Niamh Thornton. New York: Routledge, 2014. 11–23.

———. *New Latina Narrative: The Feminine Space of Postmodern Ethnicity.* Tucson: University of Arizona Press, 1999.

———. "The Postmodern Continuum of Canon and Kitsch: Narrative and Semiotic Strategies of Chicana High Culture and Chica Lit." *Multicultural and Postcolonial Narratives and Narrative Theory.* Ed. Frederick Luis Aldama. Austin: University of Texas Press, 2011. 165–81.

Miller, Laura J. *Reluctant Capitalists: Bookselling and the Culture of Consumption.* Chicago: University of Chicago Press, 2006.

Modleski, Tania. *Loving with a Vengeance: Mass-Produced Fantasies for Women.* 2nd ed. New York: Routledge, 2008.

Morrison, Amanda Maria. "Chicanas and 'Chick Lit': Contested *Latinidad* in the Novels of Alisa Valdes-Rodriguez." *Journal of Popular Culture* 43.2 (2010): 309–29.

Mukherjea, Ananya. "My Vampire Boyfriend: Postfeminism, 'Perfect' Masculinity, and the Contemporary Appeal of Paranormal Romance." *Studies in Popular Culture* 33.2 (2011): 1–20.

Negrón-Muntaner, Frances. *Boricua Pop: Puerto Ricans and the Latinization of American Culture.* New York: New York University, 2004.

Nevaer, Louis E. V. "Finding the American Dream—In Mexico." *New America Media.* 17 Mar. 2009. Web.

Ogunnaike, Lola. "Black Writers Seize Glamorous Ground around 'Chick Lit.'" *New York Times.* 31 May 2004. Web.

O'Hara, Lilia. "Go Her Own Way." *San Diego Union-Tribune.* 17 Oct. 2004. F-1.

Olcott, Jocelyn, Mary Kay Vaughan, and Gabriela Cano, eds. *Sex in Revolution: Gender, Politics, and Power in Modern Mexico.* Durham, NC: Duke University Press, 2006.

Ortega, Teresa. "Interview with Alisa Valdes-Rodriguez." 7 Apr. 2009. *AfterEllen.* Web.

Pettman, Dominic. *Love and Other Technologies: Retrofitting Eros for the Information Age.* Bronx, NY: Fordham University Press, 2006.

Philips, Deborah. "Shopping for Men: The Single Woman Narrative." *Women: A Cultural Review* 11.3 (2000): 238–51.

Potts, Tracey. "'Walking the Line': Kitsch, Class and the Morphing Subject of Value." *Nottingham Modern Languages Publications Archive.* Nottingham, UK: University of Nottingham, 2007. Web.

Radway, J. A. *Reading the Romance: Women, Patriarchy, and Popular Literature*. Chapel Hill: University of North Carolina Press. 1984.

Ramírez, Catherine. "The End of Chicanismo: Alisa Valdes-Rodriguez's *Dirty Girls*." Research Report no. 2. Los Angeles: University of California–Los Angeles Chicano/Latino Research Center, n.d. 1–41.

"Reading Guide: *The Feminist and the Cowboy*, Alisa Valdes." *Penguin*. Penguin Group, n.d. Web. 5 July 2014.

Rios, Lara. *Becoming Americana*. New York: Berkley Books, 2006.

———. *Becoming Latina in 10 Easy Steps*. New York: Berkley Books, 2006.

———. "Meet Lara." *Lara-Rios.com*. n.d. Web. 8 Apr. 2009.

———. "What Is the American Dream?" *Lara's Scratch Pad*. n.d. Web. 7 Apr. 2009.

"Romance Industry Statistics." *Romance Writers of America*. n.d. Web. 7 July 2014.

Rosaldo, Renata. "Cultural Citizenship, Inequality, and Multiculturalism." *Latino Cultural Citizenship: Claiming Identity, Space, and Rights*. Ed. William Vincent Flores and Rina Benmayor. Boston: Beacon Press, 1997. 27–38.

Saldívar, Ramón. "Imagining Cultures: The Transnational Imaginary in Postrace America." *Journal of Transnational American Studies* 4.2 (2012): 1–18.

Sammons, Jeffrey. "The Bildungsroman for Nonspecialists: An Attempt at a Clarification." *Reflection and Action: Essays on the Bildungsroman*. Ed. James Hardin. Columbia: University of South Carolina Press, 1991. 26–45.

Sánchez, George. "'Go after the Women'—Americanization and the Mexican Immigrant Woman, 1915–1929." In *Stanford Center for Chicano Research*. Working paper no. 6, 1984. 1–34.

Sloan, Kathryn A. *Runaway Daughters: Seduction, Elopement, and Honor in Nineteenth-Century Mexico*. Albuquerque: University of New Mexico, 2002.

Smith, Caroline. *Cosmopolitan Consumerism and Chick Lit*. New York: Routledge, 2008.

Sommer, Doris. *Foundational Fictions: The National Romances of Latin America*. Berkeley: University of California Press, 1993.

Taylor, Charles. *Modern Social Imaginaries*. Durham, NC: Duke University Press, 2004.

Tulabut, Erlina. "Chica Lit." *marycastillo.com*. Web. 7 Apr. 2009.

Ulibarri, Kristy. "Neoliberalism." *The Routledge Companion to Latino/a Literature*. Ed. Suzanne Bost and Frances R. Aparicio. New York: Routledge, 2013. 152–62.

Uzendoski, Andrew. "Chica(no) Lit: Reappropriating Adorno's Washing Machine in Nina Marie Martínez's ¡Caramba!" MA thesis. University of Texas at Austin, 2010.

Valdes, Alisa. *Dirty Girls on Top*. New York: St. Martin's Griffin, 2008.

———. *Dirty Girls Social Club*. New York: St. Martin's Griffin, 2003.

———. *Lauren's Saints of Dirty Faith*. Amazon CreateSpace: Alisa Valdes-Rodriguez, 2010.

———. *Playing with Boys*. New York: St. Martin's Griffin, 2005.

———. *Puta: An Erotic Coming of Age Novel*. Amazon CreateSpace: Alisa Valdes-Rodriguez, 2013.

Valdéz, Zulema. *The New Entrepreneurs: How Race, Class and Gender Shape American Enterprise*. Stanford, CA: Stanford University Press, 2011.

Vallejo, Jody. *From Barrios to Burbs: The Making of the Mexican American Middle Class*. Stanford, CA: Stanford University Press, 2012.

Weaver, Teresa K. "'Dirty Girls': Author Balks at 'Latina' Writer Label." *Atlanta-Journal Constitution*. 23 June 2003. F-1D.

Wendell, Sarah, and Candy Tam. *Beyond Heaving Bosoms: The Smart Bitches' Guide to Romance Novels*. New York: Simon and Schuster, 2009.

Wentz, Laurel. "Kitsch Is Key to Apparel Maker's Branding Effort: Mexico's NaCo Appeals to Hispanics, and Macy's, by Mocking Latino Tackiness." *Advertising Age Hispanic*. 30 July 2007. Web.

Wixon, Lisa M. "Cuba for Dummies." *Washington Post*. 6 Aug. 2006. Web.

———. *Dirty Blonde and Half-Cuban*. New York: HarperCollins, 2005.

Young, Erin S. "Flexible Heroines, Flexible Narratives: The Werewolf Romances of Kelley Armstrong and Carrie Vaughn." *Extrapolation* 52.2 (2011): 204–26.

Index